Introduction to Personal Computers Using Microsoft® Windows® 8

Introduction to Personal Computers Using Microsoft® Windows® 8

Part Number: 091117
Course Edition: 2.0

Acknowledgements

PROJECT TEAM

Author	Media Designer	Content Editor
Jan Prescott	Alex Tong	Joe McElveney

Notices

DISCLAIMER

While Logical Operations, Inc. takes care to ensure the accuracy and quality of these materials, we cannot guarantee their accuracy, and all materials are provided without any warranty whatsoever, including, but not limited to, the implied warranties of merchantability or fitness for a particular purpose. The name used in the data files for this course is that of a fictitious company. Any resemblance to current or future companies is purely coincidental. We do not believe we have used anyone's name in creating this course, but if we have, please notify us and we will change the name in the next revision of the course. Logical Operations is an independent provider of integrated training solutions for individuals, businesses, educational institutions, and government agencies. Use of screenshots, photographs of another entity's products, or another entity's product name or service in this book is for editorial purposes only. No such use should be construed to imply sponsorship or endorsement of the book by, nor any affiliation of such entity with Logical Operations. This courseware may contain links to sites on the Internet that are owned and operated by third parties (the "External Sites"). Logical Operations is not responsible for the availability of, or the content located on or through, any External Site. Please contact Logical Operations if you have any concerns regarding such links or External Sites.

TRADEMARK NOTICES

Logical Operations and the Logical Operations logo are trademarks of Logical Operations Corporation and its affiliates.

Microsoft® Windows® 8 is a registered trademark of Microsoft Corporation in the U.S. and other countries. The Microsoft products and services discussed or described may be trademarks or registered trademarks of Microsoft Corporation. All other product and service names used may be common law or registered trademarks of their respective proprietors.

Copyright © 2012 Logical Operations, Inc. All rights reserved. Screenshots used for illustrative purposes are the property of the software proprietor. This publication, or any part thereof, may not be reproduced or transmitted in any form or by any means, electronic or mechanical, including photocopying, recording, storage in an information retrieval system, or otherwise, without express written permission of Logical Operations, 500 Canal View Boulevard, Rochester, NY 14623, 1-800-456-4677 in the United States and Canada, 1-585-350-7000 in all other countries. Logical Operations' World Wide Web site is located at **www.logicaloperations.com**.

This book conveys no rights in the software or other products about which it was written; all use or licensing of such software or other products is the responsibility of the user according to terms and conditions of the owner. Do not make illegal copies of books or software. If you believe that this book, related materials, or any other Logical Operations materials are being reproduced or transmitted without permission, please call 1-800-456-4677 in the United States and Canada, 1-585-350-7000 in all other countries.

Introduction to Personal Computers Using Microsoft® Windows® 8

Getting to Know PCs and the Windows 8 User Interface.................. 1
    Identify Components of a Personal Computer........................2
    Sign In to Windows 8..6
    Navigate the Start Screen...12

Using Modern Apps and Navigation Features............................. 23
    Access and Identify the Charms..24
    Modern Apps and Common Navigation Features....................28
    Multitasking with Apps...34

Working with Desktop Applications.. 41
    Navigate the Desktop... 42
    Manage Files and Folders with File Explorer..........................49
    Elements of a Desktop Window...58
    Create and Modify Files with Desktop Applications................ 65

Using Internet Explorer 10...75
    Navigate Internet Explorer 10...76
    Browse the Web...82

Customizing the Windows 8 Environment.................................. 93
    Customize the Start Screen..94
    Customize the Desktop... 104

Using Windows 8 Security Features... 113
Set Privacy Levels and Passwords.. 114
Use Windows Defender.. 122
Store and Share Files with SkyDrive.. 126

Appendix A: Other Windows 8 Features.. 135
Create a New User Account.. 136
File History.. 137

Lesson Labs.. 139

Solutions.. 145

Glossary... 147

Index... 149

About This Course

Welcome to Introduction to Personal Computers Using Microsoft® Windows® 8. Whether you're new to computers or have used them in the past, this class will help you become more comfortable using a personal computer (PC) and, more specifically, the Windows 8 interface. This course will help you to define what a PC is, and familiarize you with the Windows 8 user interface and its basic capabilities. In this course, you will explore Windows 8 and learn how to create documents, send email, browse the Internet, and share information between applications and with other users.

Course Description

Target Student
This course is designed for any end user who is interested in learning about and using the features and functionality of the Windows 8 operating system for personal and/or professional use.

Course Prerequisites
This course is intended for new computer users who want to use the basic tools and features of Windows 8. No particular prerequisite skills are required, but any previous exposure to personal computers and the Internet is helpful.

Course Objectives
Upon successful completion of this course, you will be able to perform basic work-related tasks on a PC running the Windows 8 operating system.

You will:

- Navigate the Windows 8 and Desktop environments.
- Manage files and folders.
- Use programs and tools provided by Windows 8.
- Browse the Internet.
- Customize the Windows 8 Start screen and Desktop.
- Use Windows 8 security features.

The LogicalCHOICE Home Screen
The LogicalCHOICE Home screen is your entry point to the LogicalCHOICE learning experience, of which this course manual is only one part. Visit the LogicalCHOICE Course screen both during and after class to make use of the world of support and instructional resources that make up the LogicalCHOICE experience.

Log-on and access information for your LogicalCHOICE environment will be provided with your class experience. On the LogicalCHOICE Home screen, you can access the LogicalCHOICE Course screens for your specific courses.

Each LogicalCHOICE Course screen will give you access to the following resources:

- eBook: an interactive electronic version of the printed book for your course.
- LearnTOs: brief animated components that enhance and extend the classroom learning experience.

Depending on the nature of your course and the choices of your learning provider, the LogicalCHOICE Course screen may also include access to elements such as:

- The interactive eBook.
- Social media resources that enable you to collaborate with others in the learning community using professional communications sites such as LinkedIn or microblogging tools such as Twitter.
- Checklists with useful post-class reference information.
- Any course files you will download.
- The course assessment.
- Notices from the LogicalCHOICE administrator.
- Virtual labs, for remote access to the technical environment for your course.
- Your personal whiteboard for sketches and notes.
- Newsletters and other communications from your learning provider.
- Mentoring services.
- A link to the website of your training provider.
- The LogicalCHOICE store.

Visit your LogicalCHOICE Home screen often to connect, communicate, and extend your learning experience!

How to Use This Book

As You Learn

This book is divided into lessons and topics, covering a subject or a set of related subjects. In most cases, lessons are arranged in order of increasing proficiency.

The results-oriented topics include relevant and supporting information you need to master the content. Each topic has various types of activities designed to enable you to practice the guidelines and procedures as well as to solidify your understanding of the informational material presented in the course. Procedures and guidelines are presented in a concise fashion along with activities and discussions. Information is provided for reference and reflection in such a way as to facilitate understanding and practice.

Data files for various activities as well as other supporting files for the course are available by download from the LogicalCHOICE Course screen. In addition to sample data for the course exercises, the course files may contain media components to enhance your learning and additional reference materials for use both during and after the course.

At the back of the book, you will find a glossary of the definitions of the terms and concepts used throughout the course. You will also find an index to assist in locating information within the instructional components of the book.

As You Review

Any method of instruction is only as effective as the time and effort you, the student, are willing to invest in it. In addition, some of the information that you learn in class may not be important to you immediately, but it may become important later. For this reason, we encourage you to spend some time reviewing the content of the course after your time in the classroom.

As a Reference

The organization and layout of this book make it an easy-to-use resource for future reference. Taking advantage of the glossary, index, and table of contents, you can use this book as a first source of definitions, background information, and summaries.

Course Icons

Watch throughout the material for these visual cues:

Icon	Description
	A **Note** provides additional information, guidance, or hints about a topic or task.
	A **Caution** helps make you aware of places where you need to be particularly careful with your actions, settings, or decisions so that you can be sure to get the desired results of an activity or task.
	LearnTO notes show you where an associated LearnTO is particularly relevant to the content. Access LearnTOs from your LogicalCHOICE Course screen.
	Checklists provide job aids you can use after class as a reference to performing skills back on the job. Access checklists from your LogicalCHOICE Course screen.
	Social notes remind you to check your LogicalCHOICE Course screen for opportunities to interact with the LogicalCHOICE community using social media.
	Notes Pages are intentionally left blank for you to write on.

1 | Getting to Know PCs and the Windows 8 User Interface

Lesson Time: 45 minutes

Lesson Objectives

In this lesson, you will:

- Identify components of a personal computer.
- Sign in to Windows 8.
- Explore the Windows 8 Modern User Interface.

Lesson Introduction

In your office and home, you work with data and know that computers can make handling that data faster and easier. You want to use a computer, but may not know where to start. Using a computer without the basic knowledge of its components and how they work together can be frustrating and can seem complicated. In this lesson, you will learn about personal computers, their components, and how these components work together; some fundamental computing concepts and basic computer terms; and how to sign in to Windows® 8. With this knowledge, you'll have a better understanding of how computers work and how they can help you become more efficient in your job.

http://www.lo-choice.com

TOPIC A

Identify Components of a Personal Computer

Learning about the different parts that make up a personal computer (PC), is a fundamental task. By identifying the different components and becoming more familiar with how they work together, you'll become more comfortable working with PCs, making learning how to use them more fun.

Personal Computers

PCs have been around since the 1970s. As technology has improved, PCs have gotten smaller and more portable, and the ways they are used more varied. Along with the traditional desktop models, personal computers can now be found in laptop and tablet form. Because it's inconvenient to carry around a keyboard and a mouse, other input methods have been developed, including voice commands and touch screens.

Unlike a mainframe computer, which is designed to be used simultaneously by many people and requires an operator to oversee its functions, PCs are small, relatively inexpensive machines designed for individual use. They can be used for creating documents, spreadsheets, and databases; or for sending and receiving email; browsing the web; playing games; and a host of other activities. In the business world, PCs can enhance your productivity by enabling you to perform business-related tasks quickly.

Although PCs come in desktop, laptop, and tablet models, they all have certain things in common. Each is made up of three components: hardware, software, and operating system (OS).

Hardware

The hardware of a computer is the physical equipment that you can touch. Hardware includes input devices (such as a keyboard or mouse), processing devices (the system unit), data storage devices (hard drives), and output devices (such as a monitor or printer). On a desktop model, these components are separate units. For laptops and tablets, the monitor, input, and processing devices are all contained in one unit. External data storage devices such as portable hard drives, Secure Digital (SD) cards, or flash drives are also hardware.

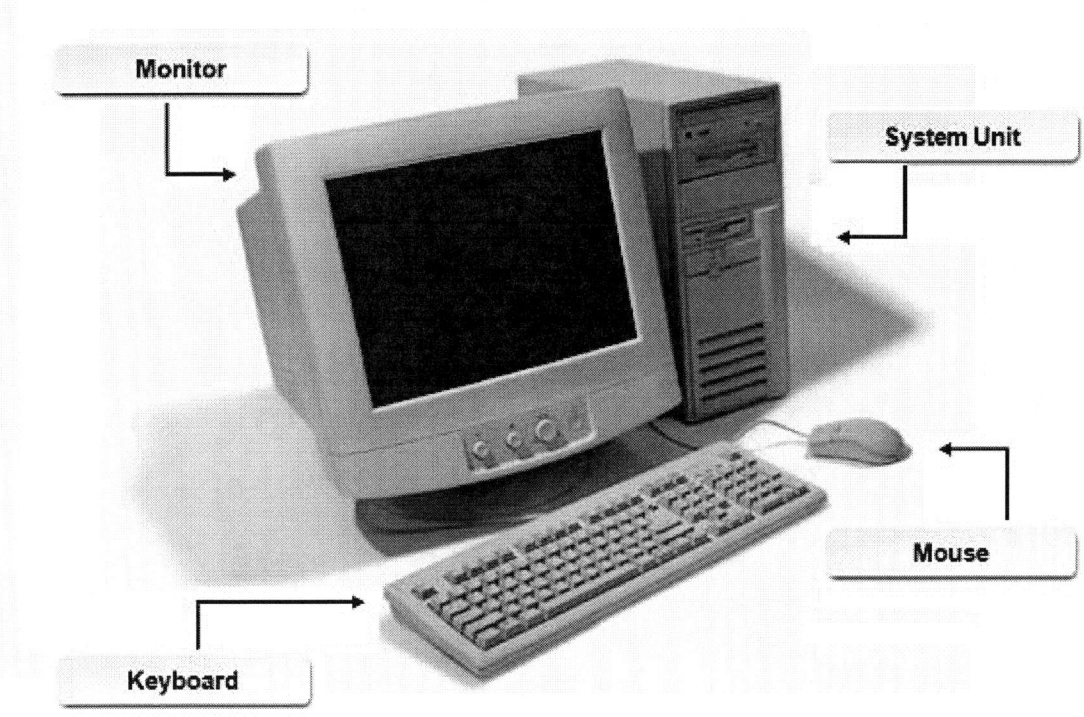

Figure 1-1: A typical desktop PC.

 Note: This course assumes that you are using a PC or tablet with a typical keyboard and mouse. At your job, if you are using a tablet or PC that uses a touch screen, you can use your fingers to make gestures on the display to perform various input tasks.

OS

Computer software is a program, or set of instructions, that enables your computer to perform specific tasks. Your computer uses two kinds of software: the operating system, and application software. The OS is the most fundamental software that creates the working environment on which application software runs. The OS manages hardware resources by interpreting input from your keyboard, mouse, or touch screen; it stores and retrieves information; and controls output devices such as the monitor or printer. Application programs require an operating system in order to work. Windows 8 is an operating system. Other operating systems used on personal computers include Windows 7, Mac OS X®, and Linux. Mobile devices such as smartphones have specialized operating systems such as Android™ from Google and iOS from Apple®.

Application Software

Application software (sometimes called simply an "*app*" on mobile devices such as smartphones and tablet computers) runs on top of the OS and is any program designed to help you perform specific tasks. For example, if you wanted to create a document, you would use a word processor, such as Microsoft® Word. There are applications designed to help you to create spreadsheets, develop graphics presentations, track accounting, keep track of your payroll, or browse the Internet. Some applications come preloaded on a new computer; others you can purchase either individually or bundled together. Typical business suite bundles include a word processor, spreadsheet, and presentation software.

The following table details common software application types and some example products.

Application	Used For	Examples
Word processor	Creating and editing documents such as letters and reports.	Microsoft Word OpenOffice Writer Quickoffice® Pro HD Corel® WordPerfect® X6
Spreadsheet	Performing accounting tasks and numerical analysis. Set up in table form with rows and columns, each cell in the table can contain text, numbers, or formulas for automatic calculation based on the contents of other cells.	Microsoft Excel® Lotus® 1-2-3® OpenOffice Calc
Database	Organizing and managing large collections of data (information); used for such things as mailing lists, billing, and other activities that require fast sorting or searching through large amounts of information.	Microsoft Access® Oracle® MySQL FileMaker® Pro
Presentation	Visually displaying information. Using graphic images, you can create slide shows, transparencies, posters, and banners. Also used for creating illustrations for use within other documents.	Microsoft PowerPoint® Lotus Freelance Graphics® Corel Presentations
Web browser	Searching, retrieving, and viewing documents, videos, images, and other content on the World Wide Web (the Internet).	Windows Internet Explorer Google Chrome™ Mozilla® Firefox®
Email	Sending and receiving digital mail messages over the Internet or other computer networks.	Microsoft Hotmail® Yahoo!® Google Gmail™ AOL®
Instant messaging	Exchanging digital, text-based messages in real time over the Internet.	Windows Messenger Yahoo! Messenger Google Talk™ AOL Instant Messenger (AIM®)

ACTIVITY 1-1
Identifying Personal Computer Components and Applications

Scenario
You are the Director of Events for Bit by Bit Fitness, a chain of sporting goods stores founded 25 years ago in Greene City, RL. Bit by Bit Fitness now has multiple fitness centers in 3 additional states: Connecticut, New York, and Vermont. Part of your job is coordinating 5k races in the cities in which Bit by Bit has stores, and keeping tabs on upcoming trends in sportswear. Your team has conducted surveys of your customers, and you want to work with the data gathered. You need to determine what applications you will use to accomplish various tasks as you process the surveys.

1. Which type of software would be best for gathering and sorting through the large amount of data contained in the surveys? Why?
   - ○ Spreadsheet
   - ○ Word processor
   - ○ Database
   - ○ Presentation

2. If you want to type up a report and create a slide show, which two types of software would you use?
   - ☐ Spreadsheet
   - ☐ Word processor
   - ☐ Database
   - ☐ Presentation

3. What is the purpose of the operating system?
   - ○ To create spreadsheets
   - ○ To create a work environment for application software
   - ○ To process data from a database
   - ○ To share data in documents

4. How are desktop PCs, laptops, and tablets similar?

5. How are desktop PCs, laptops, and tablets different?

6. What types of applications might you use for your daily work?

TOPIC B

Sign In to Windows 8

Windows 8 is designed to protect your data by using individual accounts and requiring password access to those accounts. Each time you turn on your PC, you must enter your password to access your account. By keeping your password secret, you can limit who has access to your data. Today, many companies require their employees to keep their PCs secure using passwords. With that in mind, let's get started and explore Windows 8, which has already been installed on your computer.

The Boot Process

The first thing you need to do is locate the power button on your computer to turn it on. When you turn on the PC, it performs a series of self-tests to see if everything is in working order, then it loads the OS. This is called *booting* the PC. There are times, such as when software or system updates are needed, when the PC needs to be turned off and on again to apply the updates and go through any necessary clean up procedures. This process of turning the PC off and on again is called a *reboot*.

The Lock Screen

By default, the **Lock** screen is displayed when Windows 8 finishes loading, when the PC resumes from sleep mode, or when you need to temporarily secure the PC. The **Lock** screen uses graphics to quickly present information, including time, date, Internet connection, and notifications from apps such as Mail and Calendar. You don't perform any work on the **Lock** screen—it merely acts as an informative display when you are signed out of your account and the PC is still on.

To save battery life and to prevent unauthorized people from accessing your computer, your PC is set to go into sleep mode, or time out, after being idle for a specified amount of time. When this happens, your account is temporarily locked and the **Lock** screen is displayed. Selecting anywhere on the screen will take you to the **Sign I n** screen, where you can sign in to your account and use your PC.

 Note: You can change the background of the **Lock** screen as well as change which apps display status notifications. Personalizing the **Lock** screen will be covered later in the course.

Figure 1-2: The Windows 8 Lock screen.

The Sign In Screen

Imagine you work in the payroll department. You have a lot of very sensitive data on your PC, and you want to be able to protect that data from people who should not have access to it. By requiring you to enter a password before being able to use the computer, the **Sign In** screen provides a means of preventing others from accessing your data. The **Sign In** screen also gives you the opportunity to change user accounts (if there are multiple user accounts on the PC), shut the computer down, or turn on accessibility aids to make the computer easier to use.

If more than one person uses a PC, there may be multiple accounts on it, and moving from the **Lock** screen will not take you directly to the **Sign In** screen. Instead, you will see the **Accounts Available** screen, which shows Account IDs for all of the accounts on your PC. If this is the case, select the **Account ID** that is associated with your account. This will display the **Sign In** screen for your account.

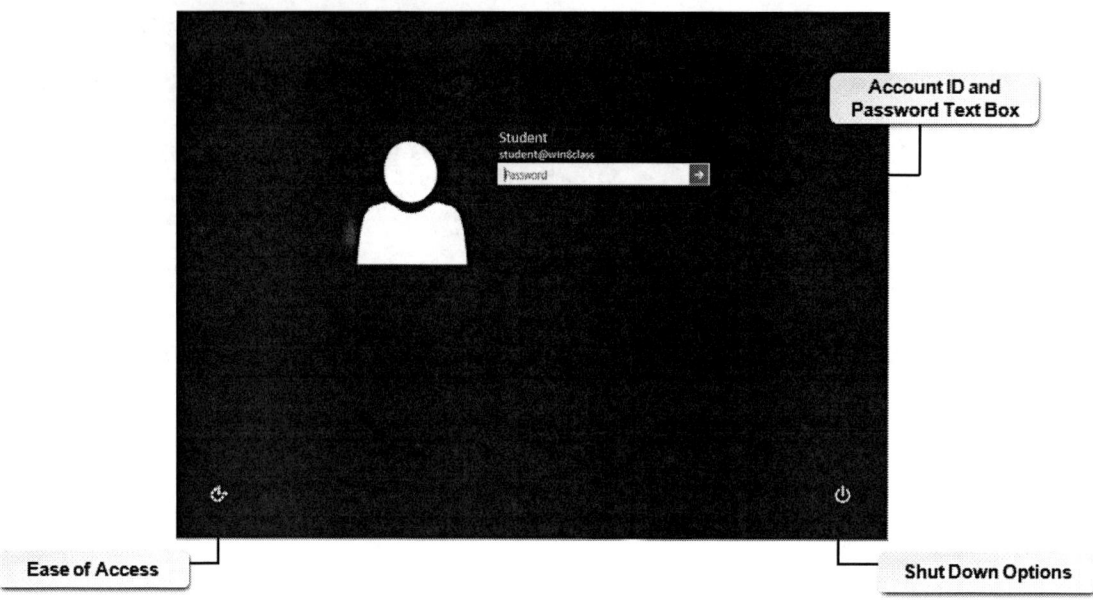

Figure 1-3: The Windows 8 Sign In screen.

Ease of Access Menu

The **Ease of Access** menu provides a way to make your computer more accessible through assistive technology. With **Ease of Access**, you can have the **Narrator** feature read aloud the text on your screen; increase the size of the page for readability; turn on an onscreen keyboard; or access other functions that offer alternative methods of making things easier to see and use.

The following table describes the features on the **Ease of Access** menu.

Ease of Access Menu Choice	Description
Narrator	**Narrator** will read aloud what is on the screen, including text that you are typing, contents of the active window, and menu options. This option is very helpful for the visually impaired. **Narrator** may not work with all applications.
Magnifier	**Magnifier** will enlarge the whole screen, or portions of the screen, to make viewing easier.
On-Screen Keyboard	Places a virtual keyboard on the screen. Useful for touch screen PCs or when a keyboard is not available.
High Contrast	Provides a darker background to make text and images stand out for better viewing.
Sticky Keys	Sometimes two or more keys must be pressed at the same time to start an action, such as **Ctrl+Alt+Del** to display **Task Manager** or cause the computer to reboot. With the **Sticky Keys** feature turned on, you can press the keys in the combination one at a time.
Filter Keys	**Filter Keys** tells the PC how long to respond when a key is pressed and to ignore repeated keystrokes. This is helpful for users who shake, or who have difficulty pressing and lifting their fingers off of keys quickly enough when typing.

Note: To further explore the **Ease of Access** menu, you can access the LearnTO **Use the Magnifier** presentation from the **LearnTO** tile on the LogicalCHOICE Course screen.

Shut Down Options Menu

Turning off your computer incorrectly can result in lost data, damaged files, and damage to your hard drive. When your computer is shut down properly, Windows goes through the process of closing any files it was reading or writing to, ending any processes that were taking place, and properly preparing the hard drive for power loss. The Windows 8 **Shut Down** menu offers different options for correctly turning off your computer:

- **Sleep**—This option is good when you're going to be away from your computer for a short time (for instance, when you're heading out for lunch) and don't want to completely shut the PC down. In sleep mode, your computer turns off the monitor, stops the disk drive, and saves its current state in memory. Sleep mode is a good way to conserve energy and extend the life of your laptop or tablet battery.
- **Shut Down**—When you are finished with your computer and want to turn it off completely, you should use this option. It allows processes that are taking place to properly close files, store any file that is in memory, run updates, and "clean up" before closing down and turning off the power. In addition to allowing the operating system to properly close out, this also gives hardware, such as the hard drive, time to prepare before the power is removed.
- **Restart**—Restart is similar to **Shut Down,** but, instead of ending with the PC turning off, the computer goes through the clean-up process, adds any updates, and then restarts the operating system. Often, when you are loading new software or making changes to settings on your computer, you'll be asked to restart your PC.

Password Sign In

If you have access to the Internet or store valuable company or personal information on your computer, you need to protect it from the many threats in today's world. Hackers, viruses, and thieves are constantly looking to gain access to computers in order to steal information from them. Passwords are one part of the defense available on your PC. The stronger the password, the harder it is for hackers to figure it out. And, like a good lock on your house, the better your password, the more likely the thief is to give up and move on. Windows 8 requires passwords to be at least eight characters long, and they must contain at least two of the following: uppercase letters, lowercase letters, numbers, and symbols (for example, & ^ % $ #).

 Caution: You should not base passwords on something that is easily found in public records, like your birth date, or your children's names. Instead, base your password on a sentence or phrase that you can easily remember. It should contain a combination of upper- and lowercase letters, numbers, and symbols.

Alternative Passwords

Windows 8 provides two alternatives to the eight-character long password. These alternatives can be used on traditional PCs, but they are designed to make signing in on a touch screen easier. The first is the picture password. With this method, you choose a picture and "draw" three gestures on the picture, in any combination of circles, straight lines, and taps. The size and placement of the gestures on the picture become your password.

The second alternative method is a PIN code. This four-digit code is a quick and easy way to sign in to your computer and does not require that you press **Enter** at the end. The PIN is submitted automatically as soon as you put in all four digits. These alternative sign-in methods can be accessed in **PC settings,** and will be discussed later in the course.

 Access the Checklist tile on your LogicalCHOICE course screen for reference information and job aids on How to Use a Mouse and Sign In to Windows 8

ACTIVITY 1-2
Signing In to Windows 8

Before You Begin
Your instructor will provide you with a user account for your Windows 8 system. Write down your user ID and password.

User ID: _____

Password: **win8class**

 Note: You may want to keep your password handy, because you will use it again later in the course.

Scenario
It's 8 A.M. and you've just arrived in the office. You want to sign in to the computer and begin your day. You get your coffee and sit down at your computer.

---

1. Turn on your computer.
    a) Locate and press the power button.
    b) Observe the computer's startup process.

2. Sign in to Windows 8.
    a) At the **Lock** screen, select anywhere, or swipe up to move to the next screen.
    b) Once you have reached the **Sign In** screen, in the **Password** text box, type *win8class* and press **Enter**.

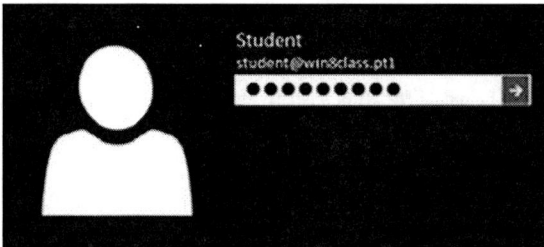

TOPIC C

Navigate the Start Screen

So far, you have identified personal computer hardware and types of software, and signed in to Windows 8. With this basic knowledge, you're ready to start putting Windows 8 to work for you.

The Start Screen

The **Start** screen is the central user interface of Windows 8 and acts as the hub from which you can access all of the capabilities of your computer. From the **Start** screen, you can run programs, check your email, add contacts, see the latest news, get updates on the weather, change the settings on your PC, sign out of your computer, go online, and much more.

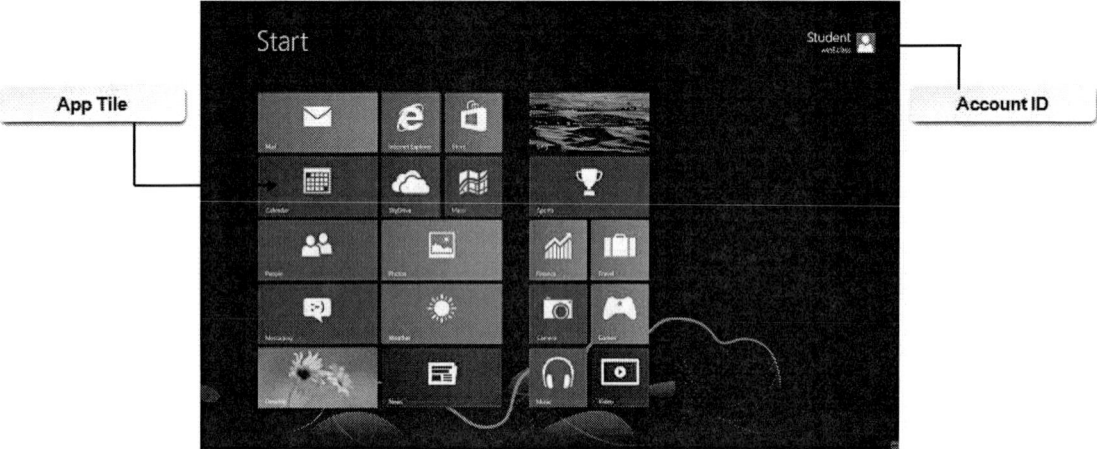

Figure 1-4: The Windows 8 Start screen.

Tiles

The first thing you'll notice about the **Start** screen is that it has colorful squares and rectangles displayed, each with a different name and picture, or icon. These colorful objects are called *tiles*, and each tile represents a different app or link to a website. The tiles aren't actually the apps themselves, but act as a shortcut or quick way of running an app. For instance, if you select the **Calendar** tile, it will run the Calendar app. If you select the **Weather** tile, you'll be taken online to view weather in any city you choose. Applications written in the new Windows 8 user interface are called *Modern apps*, while traditional software programs written for previous Windows OS versions are called *Desktop applications*. Windows 8 supports both types of software, with traditional applications running on the Desktop OS app.

Tooltips

If the name of the app is not displayed on the tile, you can hold your pointer over the tile and a *tooltip* will display the name of the app. Windows 8 also provides tooltips for icons in many of the apps.

Tile Position

As you work with Windows 8, you may find that you use some tiles more than others, or that, as you add more apps, you have so many tiles that you can't find anything. You can easily move a tile by *dragging* it to a new position. The other tiles will move to accommodate the space left by the tile you moved.

 Caution: Be careful when dragging tiles. If you press the mouse button but do not hold it down, the tile will open the app associated with it.

Live Tiles

Some tiles do more than just run apps. *Live tiles* can display real-time information, even when the app isn't running. For example, the **Finance** tile will display current stock market coverage, along with breaking financial news; the **Calendar** tile will display upcoming appointments; and the **Mail** tile will show how many unread emails you have.

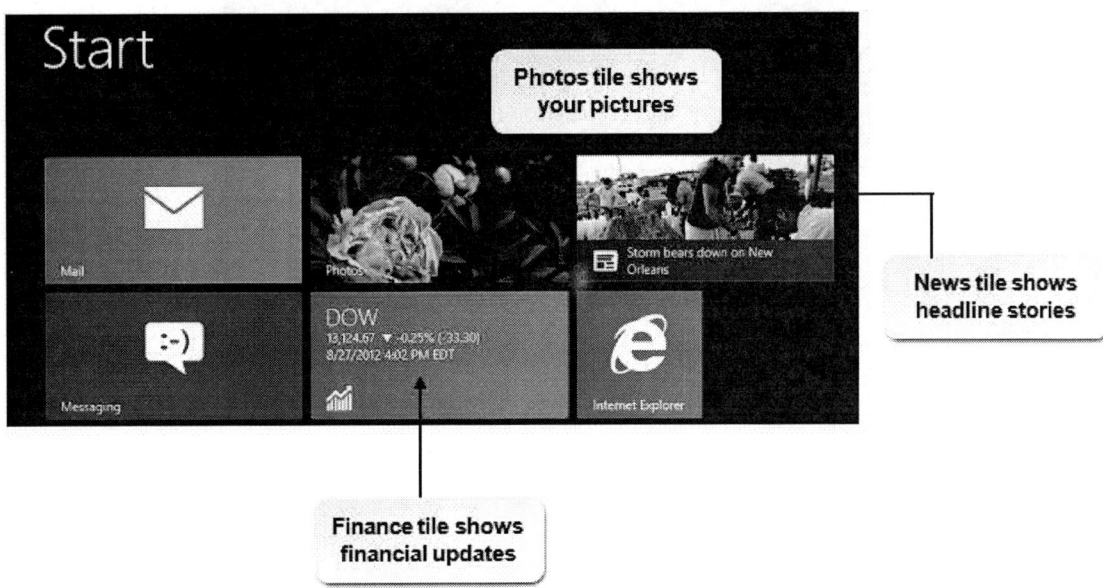

Figure 1-5: Information displayed on live tiles.

The App Command Bar

The app command bar is hidden on the bottom of the screen and contains options for managing the tiles that are currently shown on, or *pinned*, to the **Start** screen. With this command bar, you can turn a live tile on or off, unpin a tile from **Start,** uninstall an app, and change the size of a tile. Right-click the desired tile to view its app command bar.

Figure 1-6: Tile management tools on the app command bar.

The All Apps Screen

When Windows 8 is loaded on your PC, only the most commonly used apps are pinned to the **Start** screen. The **All Apps** screen allows you to view *all* of the programs available on your computer, including system commands, **Ease of Access** options, helpful apps that come bundled with

Windows 8, and any new programs that you may have installed. On the **All Apps** screen, you can run any of the programs installed on your computer, or you can pin an app to the **Start** screen, making it easier to run that app in the future. Both Modern apps and traditional applications can be pinned and unpinned to **Start**.

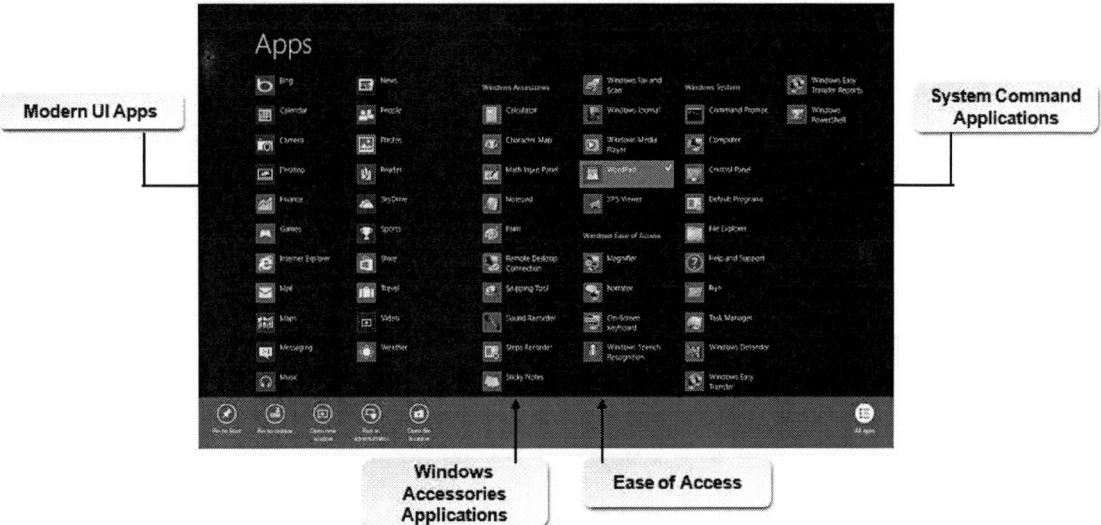

Figure 1-7: The All Apps screen with app command bar.

Start Button

You can return to the **Start** screen at any time, from any screen, by using the **Start** button. To access the **Start** button, move your pointer to the lower-left corner of your screen and select the tiny picture of the **Start** screen that appears. The **Start** button is available whenever you have navigated away from the **Start** screen. When you are on the **Start** screen, the **Start** button will take you back to the previous app you were using.

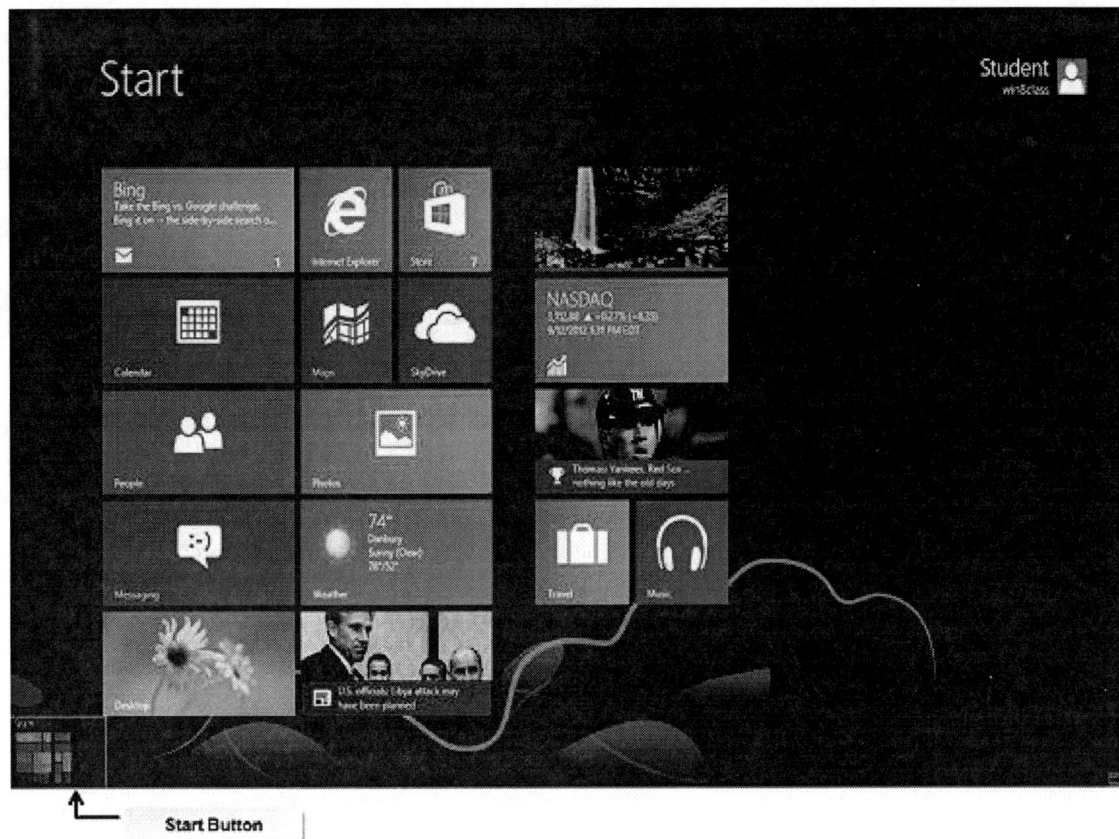

Figure 1-8: The Start button.

The Scroll Bar

The **Start** screen can hold more tiles than can be viewed on one page. You can scroll the **Start** screen in order to view all of the tiles pinned on it by using the scroll bar at the bottom of the screen. To display the scroll bar, just move your pointer and it will appear. The scroll bar has arrows on each end for slow scrolling, and a slider bar that you can drag for faster scrolling.

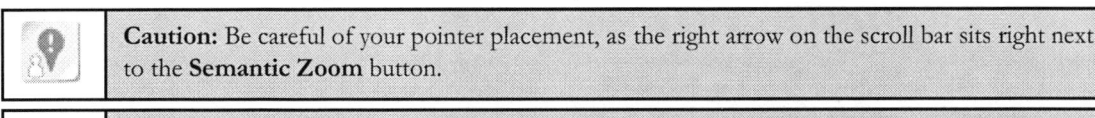

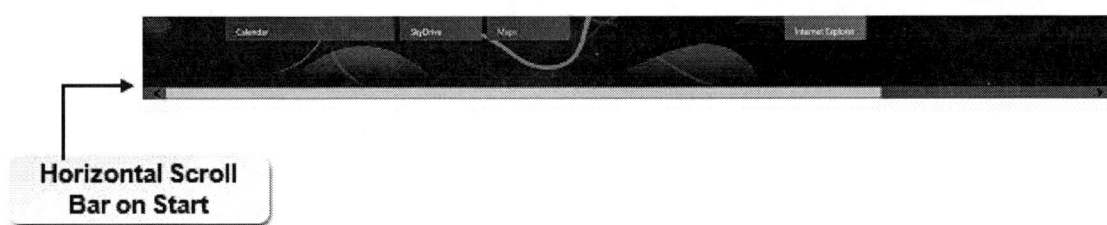

Figure 1-9: The scroll bar at the bottom of the Start screen.

ACTIVITY 1-3
Managing Tiles

Before You Begin
You are signed in to your account and are viewing the Start screen.

Scenario
You've been working with Windows 8 at your job for a while now. You really like it, but you'd like to make the tiles easier to find, and may not need all of the tiles pinned to the Start screen. You decide that taking a few minutes to manage your tiles now will save you a lot of time in your day-to-day work. Because you know you'll be too busy to use your computer for games and video, and your PC doesn't have a camera, you can unpin those tiles from the Start screen. You also don't use Finance often, but would still like to have it available, so you decide to make it smaller. It would be nice to be able to do calculations without having to get your calculator out, and you remember seeing a calculator program on the All Apps screen, so you decide to pin the calculator to the Start screen so it's always handy. Let's get started and do some housekeeping.

1. Unpin tiles from the **Start** screen.
    a) Right-click the **Games**, **Camera**, and **Video** tiles. The app command bar appears across the bottom of your screen.

    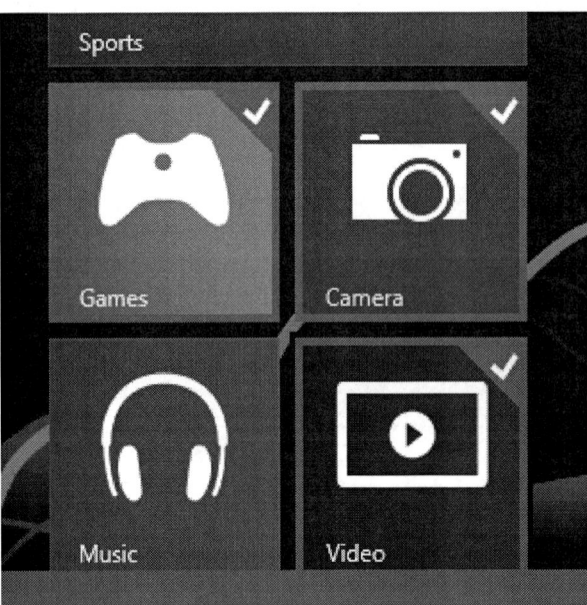

    b) On the app command bar, select **Unpin from Start**. The **Games**, **Camera**, and **Video** tiles disappear from **Start**. The tile for **Music** shifts to fill the empty space.

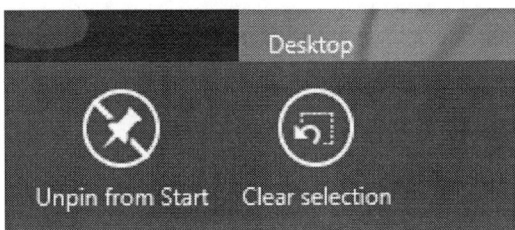

2. Change the size of a tile and move it.
   a) Right-click the **Finance** tile.
   b) On the apps command bar, select **Smaller**.

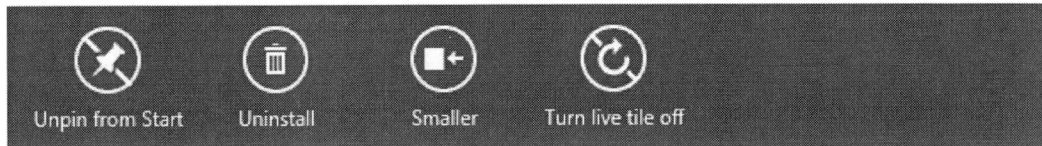

   c) Move the **Finance** tile down to the left of **Music.**

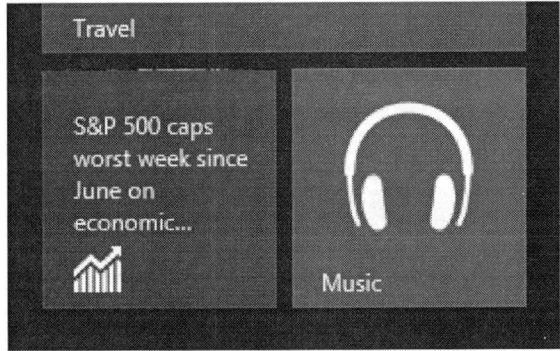

3. Pin an app to the **Start** screen.
   a) Right-click the **Start** background to display the **All Apps** command bar, and select **All Apps.**
   b) Under the **Windows Accessories** group of programs, find **Calculator** and right-click it.

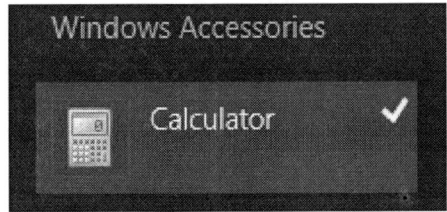

   c) On the app command bar, select **Pin to Start.**

4. Return to **Start**.
    a) Move your pointer to the lower-left corner of the screen to display the **Start** button.
    b) Select the **Start** button to return to the **Start** screen.
    c) Verify that the **Calculator** tile is now pinned to the **Start** screen.

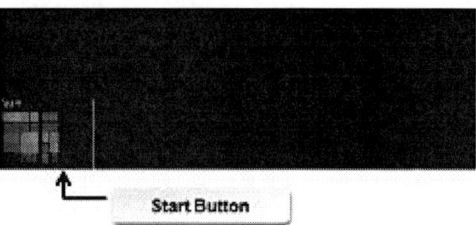

Account ID

On the top-right corner of the **Start** screen is your **Account ID**, featuring your picture and name. There may be times when you'll be sharing a computer with someone else; for instance, if your work takes you out in the field a lot, the company may supply a shared PC for those infrequent times that you and your coworkers are in the office, and each of you would be assigned an account. This enables you to customize your account with only those apps that pertain to your work, and protects your data from being changed or deleted by others. Although only one account would be active at a time, multiple people can be signed in to the computer at the same time. In these instances, it's important to know that you are using the correct account. The **Account ID** tells you whose account is currently active on the PC.

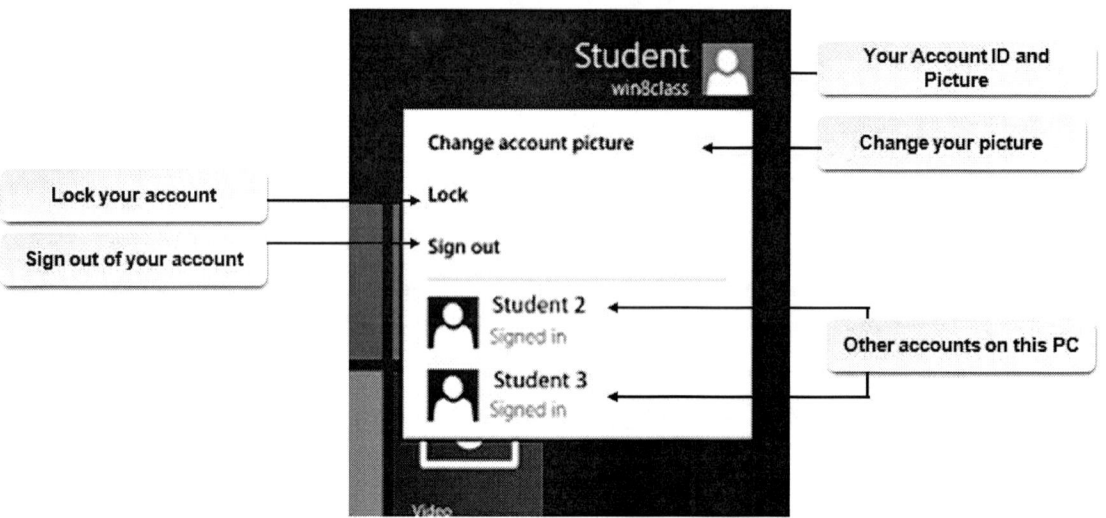

Figure 1-10: The Account ID menu.

By selecting the **Account ID,** you can access the **Account ID** menu, where you can change your account picture, lock your account, sign out of the computer, or change user accounts.

Account ID Menu Item	Description
Change account picture	Takes you to **PC settings** → **Personalize,** where you can select a picture from your files, or use the camera on your PC to create a picture as your ID. **PC settings** will be discussed later in the course.

Account ID Menu Item	Description
Lock	Leaves everything running on your account, but brings you to the **Lock** screen and locks your account. Your account cannot be accessed until your password is entered on the **Sign In** screen. Other accounts may be used while your account is locked.
Sign out	Closes all programs and files you have open and signs you out of the computer, ending your session. The PC remains on.
Other User Account ID(s)	Locks your account and lets another user sign in under their account.

 Access the Checklist tile on your LogicalCHOICE course screen for reference information and job aids on How to Lock Your Account and Sign Out of Windows 8

ACTIVITY 1-4
Using the Account ID Menu

Before You Begin
You are viewing the Start screen.

Scenario
It's the end of the day and you are ready to head home. Your company wants to save energy and has asked everyone to turn their computers off at night. You know you need to shut it down properly, and you want to practice doing it correctly. When the PC is fully shut down, you will turn it back on again to practice signing in.

1. Shut down the computer.
    a) In the upper right of your screen, select your **Account ID**.
    b) From the menu, select **Sign Out**.

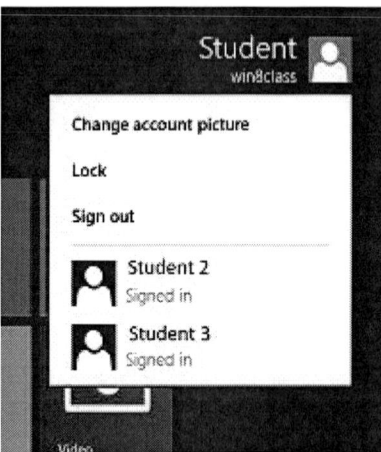

    c) At the **Lock** screen, select anywhere to get to the **Sign In** screen.
    d) At the **Sign In** screen, select the **Shut Down** icon.
    e) From the **Shut Down** menu, select **Shut Down**.
    f) When the PC is fully shut down, proceed to the next step.

2. Turn on your computer.
    a) Locate and press the power button. The computer goes through the startup process.

3. Sign in to Windows 8.
    a) At the **Lock** screen, select anywhere, or swipe up to move to the next screen.
    b) Once you have reached the **Sign In** screen, in the **Password** text box, type *win8class* and press **Enter**.

4. Lock your account.
    a) In the upper right of your screen, select your **Account ID**.
    b) From the menu, select **Lock**. Your account will be locked and you will be taken to the **Lock** screen.
    c) Sign back in to your account.

Summary

In this lesson, you identified personal computer hardware and software basics, signed in to Windows 8, and learned about the Modern User Interface. With this basic knowledge and skill, you're ready to start working with Windows 8.

Why do you think Windows 8 requires passwords to contain at least two of the following: uppercase letters, lowercase letters, numbers, and symbols? How does this benefit you?

What about the Windows 8 user interface makes using a PC easier than you thought?

 Note: Check your LogicalCHOICE Course screen for opportunities to interact with your classmates, peers, and the larger LogicalCHOICE online community about the topics covered in this course or other topics you are interested in. From the Course screen you can also access available resources for a more continuous learning experience.

http://www.lo-choice.com

2 | Using Modern Apps and Navigation Features

Lesson Time: 1 hour

Lesson Objectives

In this lesson, you will:

- Identify the Charms and explore how they can be used in various apps.
- Use the Windows 8 Start screen to open apps.
- Navigate between Modern apps.

Lesson Introduction

Now that you've seen the Microsoft® Windows® 8 Modern User Interface and explored the Start screen, it's time to use a few of the Modern apps that come bundled with Windows 8 and see how to navigate within and between them. This lesson introduces some of the basic apps that come with Windows 8 and shows how they work together and how they might make your job easier.

http://www.lo-choice.com

TOPIC A

Access and Identify the Charms

One of the design features of Windows 8 is ease of use. With the Charms, you have universal access to common tools no matter where you are in Windows 8.

The Charms

Hidden on the right side of the screen are the *Charms*. The Charms are universal tools that are available from everywhere in Windows 8, and give you access to key system-wide functions such as printing, searching, and the sharing function. Charms are dynamic and context sensitive; for instance, using the **Search Charm** within the Mail app will search through your email messages for the word or phrase you enter; using **Search** from the **Start** screen is global and will take you to the **All Apps** screen, where you can search for apps, files, and PC settings, or begin a search using an app.

Bringing up the Charms also brings up a display showing the current date and time, along with Internet connectivity strength. If you are using a laptop or tablet, it will also display battery life.

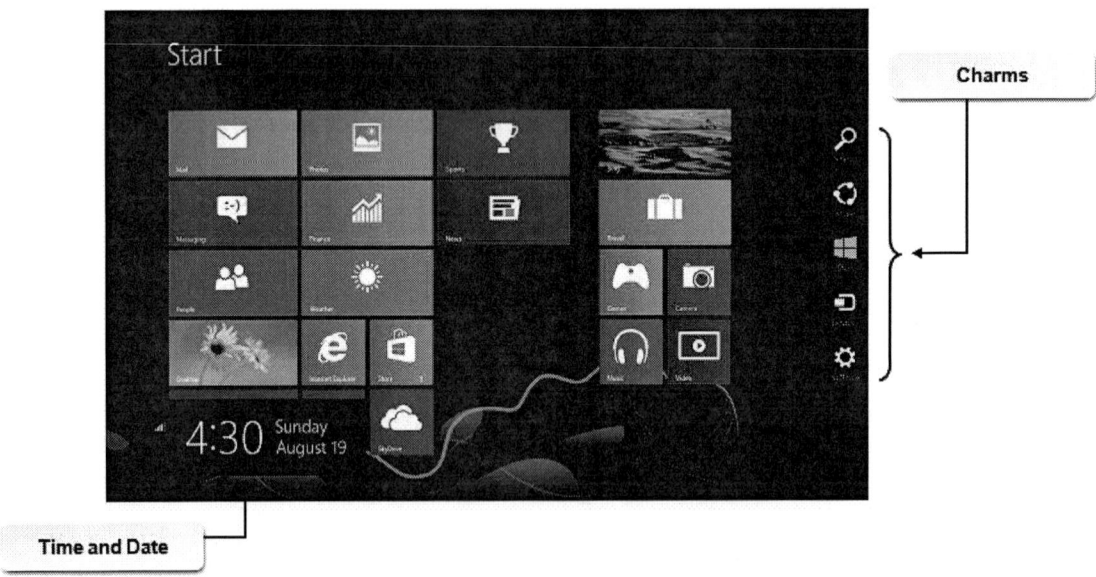

Figure 2-1: The Charms available on the Start screen.

The following table describes the Charms available on the **Start** screen.

Charm	Used For
Search	Searching for apps, settings, files, or online searches. Context sensitive and conducts searches differently depending on where you are when you access it. The **Search** menu indicates where you will be searching by listing the targeted search app above the **Search** text box, possible matches to your search will display. Some apps display suggestions below the **Search** text box. Others list suggestions to the left after text is entered. You can select these suggestions to begin the search or start the app. Search works with Modern apps, but not Desktop applications. For each app, Windows 8 saves your search phrases for use in future searches and displays them under the **Search** text box. Select one of these for faster searching.

Charm	Used For
Share	The **Share Charm** allows you to share data via Mail or any social networking site that supports the Share function. Share only works with the Modern apps that have the necessary permission. The options for sharing vary by app and type of data you are sharing.
Start	The **Start Charm** works the same way as the **Start** button and returns you to the **Start** screen from any app. Or, if you are at the **Start** screen, it will return you to the last open app you were using.
Devices	The **Devices Charm** allows you to interact with the devices connected to your PC. Using this Charm, you can connect to other devices, choose a printer and print from any Modern app, stream media and other content to external devices, and configure the monitors connected to your PC. This last option is helpful when you are working with dual monitors.
Settings	The **Settings Charm** is also context sensitive, and options vary among apps. On **Start,** it allows you to access **Help** and **PC settings**, clear any personal information from live tiles, connect to and check on the strength of your Internet connection, adjust speaker volume, change the brightness of your screen, display an onscreen keyboard, and hide notifications. This charm also enables you to access the power menu to shut down, restart, or put your PC in sleep mode.

Note: PC settings will be discussed in greater depth later in the course.

Access the Checklist tile on your LogicalCHOICE course screen for reference information and job aids on How to Access the Charms

ACTIVITY 2-1
Viewing the Charms

Before You Begin
You are viewing the Start screen.

Scenario
You have just set up your PC with Windows 8 and have familiarized yourself with the Start screen and the tiles. Now you'd like to take a look at the Charms to see what tools are available, and see how a basic search works by searching for the Mail app.

1. Access the Charms.
    a) Move your pointer to the top right of your screen and slide it down the right side to display the Charms.

     Note: If the Charms don't appear, pull your pointer away from the right side and try again. Do not press any of the mouse buttons while you're doing this.

    b) Slide your pointer over each Charm. The Charms are highlighted as your pointer moves over each one.
    c) Move your pointer to the **Start** screen, away from the Charms, to close the Charms.

2. Search for apps.
    a) Display the Charms.
    b) Select the **Search Charm** to display the **All Apps** screen. Verify that **Apps** is listed above the **Search** text box.

    c) In the **Search** text box, type *Mail*
    d) As you type, observe how the suggestions listed on the left side of your screen change as you enter each letter.

     Note: Press **Backspace** to clear the text if you make a mistake.

Note: You can use the **Search Charm** to quickly find an app not pinned to **Start,** and open the app by selecting it in the list of results.

e) In the suggestions, verify that the Mail app is listed.
f) Use the **Start** button to return to **Start.**

Note: To further explore the Search Charm, you can access the LearnTO **Search from Start** presentation from the **LearnTO** tile on the LogicalCHOICE Course screen.

TOPIC B

Modern Apps and Common Navigation Features

To get you started working, Windows 8 includes several apps. Let's take a look at some of the apps and see how to use common navigation tools.

Modern Apps

Windows 8 comes preloaded with several simple apps that can be useful and give you a good idea of how Modern apps work. Some of these apps include Mail, Calendar, People, Maps, Weather, and News. To start an app, select the tile associated with it.

Point out to students that this activity is not so much about introducing the apps bundled with Windows 8 as it is about showing techniques that apply to all Windows 8

Common App Navigation Features

Modern apps have several common navigation features, including scroll bars, app command bars, **Next Page** and **Previous Page** arrows, a **Back** arrow, onscreen content icons, and the Charms. As with the **Start** screen, apps use scroll bars to view content that can't fit on one screen. Some apps have scroll bars along the right side for vertical scrolling, or along the bottom for horizontal scrolling. Access app command bars by right-clicking the page background or a specific item on the screen. App command bars can appear at the top as well as the bottom of the screen. Command bar options vary according to the app in which they appear.

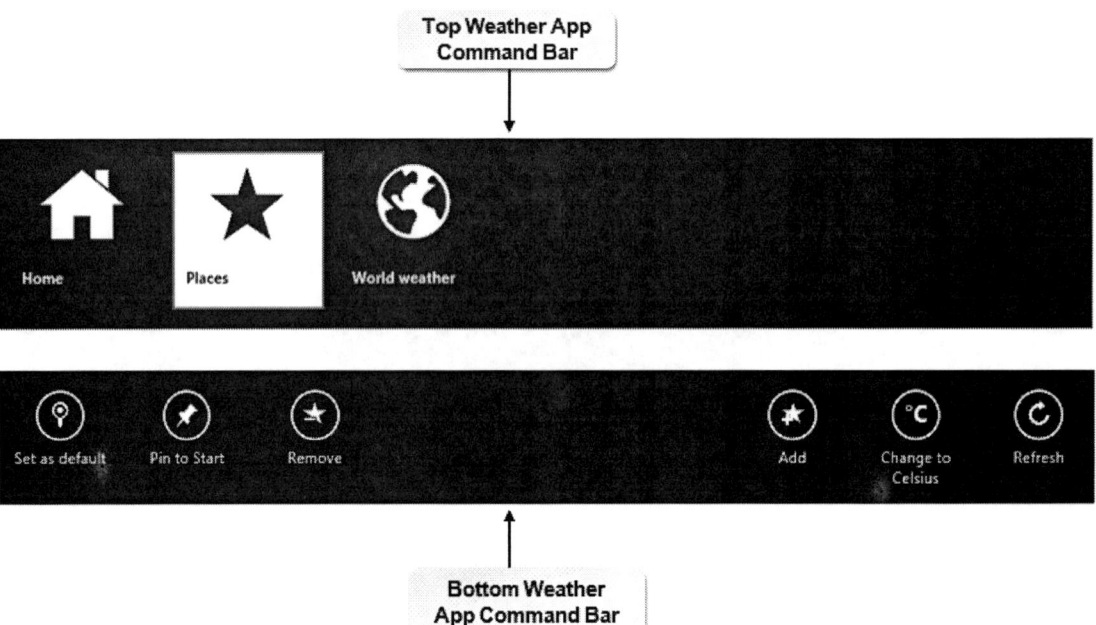

Figure 2-2: The top and bottom app command bars in Weather.

Apps often have interactive icons and tiles that change the contents of the page or reveal more information. For instance, the Weather app displays a table that will show historical temperature, precipitation, or hours of sunshine, depending on which icon you select. It also offers tiles that, when selected, will display time-elapsed weather conditions such as temperature and cloud cover. You can also find small arrows within the page that hide or reveal more information.

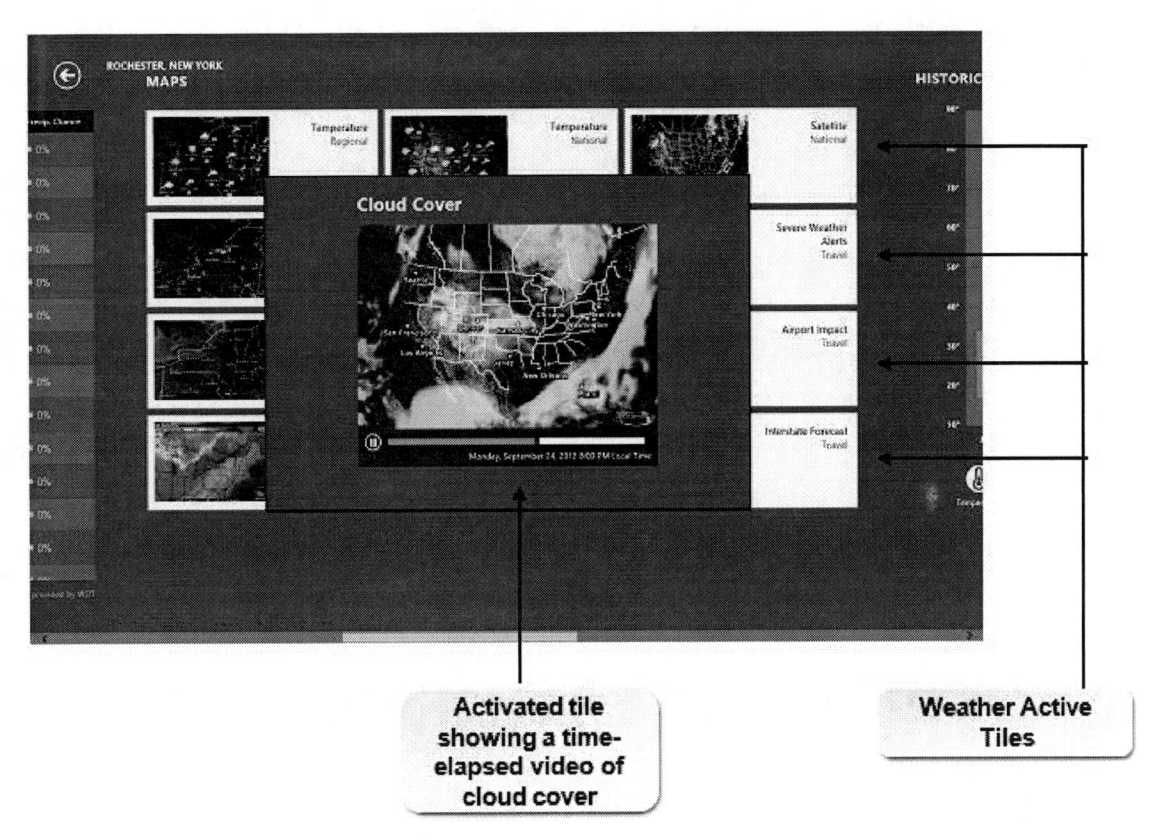

Figure 2-3: An active tile in Weather opens a video of projected cloud cover.

> Access the Checklist tile on your LogicalCHOICE course screen for reference information and job aids on How to Open a Modern App and Use Navigation Features

ACTIVITY 2-2
Navigating a Modern App

Scenario
Bit by Bit is hosting a 5k race this weekend in Danbury, CT. Because weather has a big impact on the runners and vendors, you need to be aware of any impending problems and plan accordingly. You're currently in another city, so you need to go online to check the weather forecast in Danbury to see if you'll have to order extra tents. You'd also like to check the weather in New York City for a sporting goods convention you'll be attending there tomorrow.

1. Open the Weather app.
    a) On the **Start** screen, select the **Weather** tile. The Weather app opens.
    b) If prompted, select **Allow** to let the Weather app use your location.
    c) Verify that the **Weather** screen comes up displaying the weather where you are.

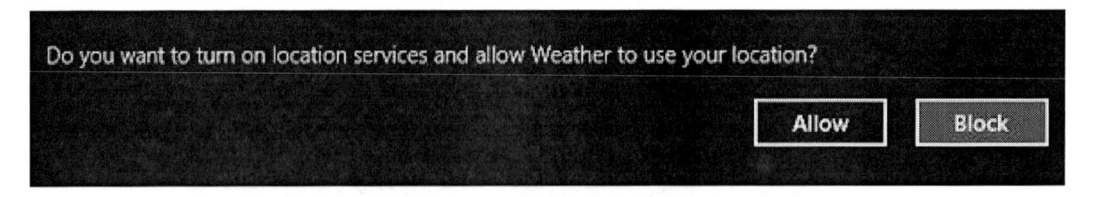

2. Search for a location.
    a) Display the Charms and select **Search**. The **Search** text box reads: Search for a city.
    b) Note that the cursor is flashing in this box, indicating that any text you type will be entered here.
    c) Verify that Weather is listed above the **Search** box, and scroll down through the list of apps below the **Search** box to see that **Weather** is highlighted.
    d) Scroll back to the top of the page.

    e) In the **Search** text box, enter *Danbury* and examine the suggested locations listed below the text box as you type. Confirm that the results are refined as you get more specific.
    f) When it shows in the list below the text box, select **Danbury, Connecticut, United States**.

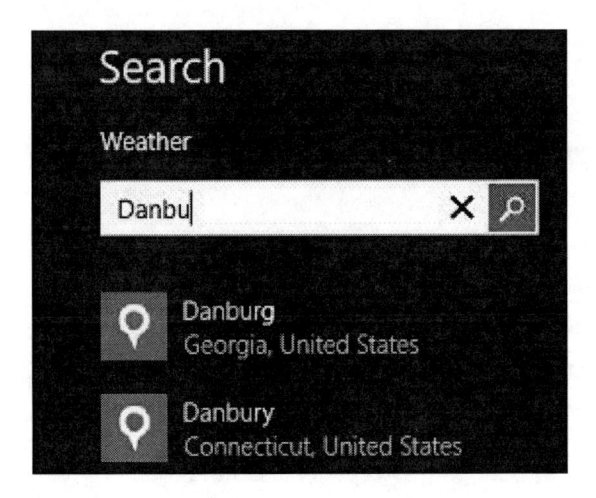

g) In the Weather app, verify that Danbury, CT weather is displayed.
h) Observe that the app command bar is open on the bottom of the page.
i) Select anywhere on the background of Weather to hide the command bar and close the **Search** pane.

3. Use navigation icons.
   a) Select the right arrow to the right of the five-day forecast to reveal forecasts for the next five days.

   b) Verify that the arrow now points to the left. This signifies that selecting it will scroll to the left, going back to the first five days of forecasts.
   c) Select the arrow and confirm that the first five days are displayed again.

   d) Below the right arrow, select the down arrow. Observe that more information is revealed below the five-day forecast.

   e) Confirm that the arrow now points up.
   f) Select the up arrow to hide the additional information.

4. Access the command bars.
   a) Right-click the page. Verify that the top and bottom app command bars are displayed.
   b) Examine the options in the top app command bar.

   > **Note:** You can use the bottom app command bar here to set the current location as the default page, pin the current location's weather to the **Start** screen, add this location as a favorite, change the display from Fahrenheit to Celsius, or refresh the page to get more current data. On the top command bar, **Home** will take you to your default location page; **Places** has links to cities you have recently viewed or set as your favorites; and **World weather** will show you temperatures for large cities around the world.

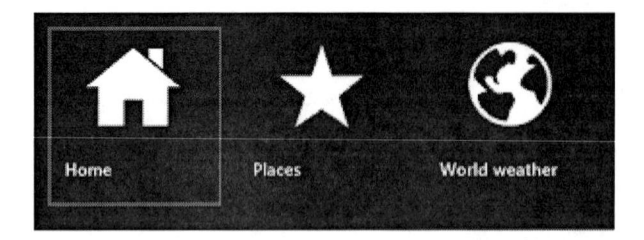

   c) Select **World weather** to display an interactive page showing the current weather in cities across the world.

5. Use interactive navigation features.
   a) Select a land area. Observe how the map zooms in on that area and weather is displayed for cities in that region.
   b) Select the map again to zoom back out.
   c) Select the **New York City** weather label. Confirm the weather is displayed for New York City.

6. Navigate to the previous page.
   a) In the top-left corner, select the **Back** arrow to go back a page. Repeat until you are back to the Danbury weather page.

7. Set a default Weather home page.
   a) From the app command bar, select **Places.** Verify that Danbury is listed as a recent weather search.
   b) Right-click the **Danbury** tile.
   c) On the command bar, select **Set as default.**

8. Add a favorite Place.
   a) Select the black tile with the plus sign.
   b) In the text box that appears, enter **New York City** and press **Enter**.
   c) Under **Favorites,** verify that New York City is now listed.

9. Return to the default Weather page.
   a) Select the top tile to return to the default Weather page.

10. Return to **Start.**

TOPIC C

Multitasking with Apps

In your daily work, you probably won't be using one program at a time, but will open multiple programs to reference information from one program for use in another, or to multitask for more efficiency. With this in mind, Windows 8 was designed to make moving from one app to another easy.

Multiple-App Functionality

It's often useful to work with multiple apps, such as when you are referring to information in one app for use in another, or when you are called away from the document you are working on to display information for a coworker. Windows 8 supports running more than one app at a time, and Modern apps are designed to work together. The method for opening a second app is the same as opening the first: selecting the appropriate tile on the **Start** screen. The app you are currently working with typically runs in the foreground, covering the entire screen, while any other open app is suspended in the background to conserve energy. When you switch to the suspended app, it instantly resumes running, and the app you were working with is suspended. There are exceptions to this rule. For instance, the Music app continues running in the background so that you can listen to music as you work. Windows 8 also provides for viewing two apps at the same time.

The Switcher

When you have more than one app running at a time, the *Switcher* lets you flip between them. Hidden in the top-left corner of your screen, the **Switcher** will show a tile of the previous app you were working with. Select the tile to switch to the suspended app. If there are more than two apps running, you can select the **Switcher** multiple times until you get to your app, or you can slide your pointer down the left side to display tiles for all apps that are currently open. Select any of these to resume working in the app represented by that tile.

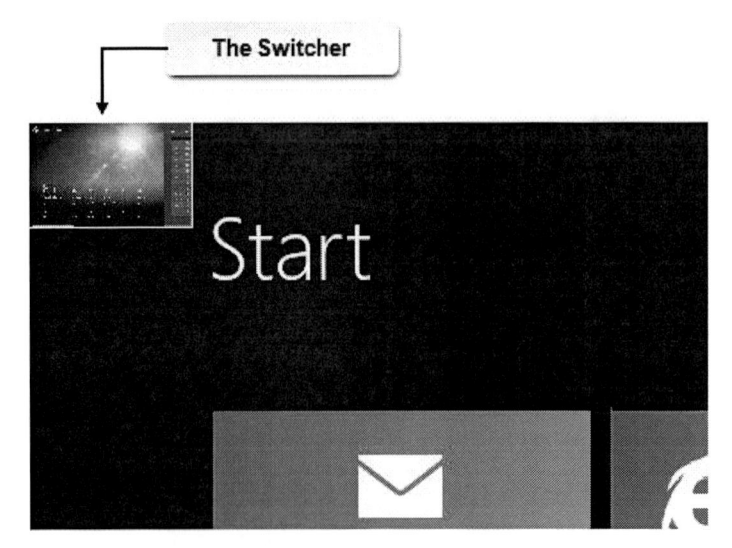

Figure 2-4: The Switcher showing the Weather tile.

The Snap Feature

There may be instances when you'll want to view two apps at the same time. Perhaps you're working with figures on a spreadsheet and need to include some of these in a report or email. Rather than having to remember the numbers as you flip between the apps, you can use the *Snap* feature to show both apps on the screen together. To do this, just move your pointer to the top of the page and drag the app to the side. The app will "snap" into a pane, leaving a second pane to display another app. Use the **Switcher** to put the second app into the other pane. The main app will cover three quarters of the page, while the secondary app will display on the remaining quarter. You can easily switch this distribution by dragging the *snap bar* to the left or right as needed. To return any app to suspension and display only one app on your screen, drag the snap bar all the way to the left or right, covering up the app you wish to suspend.

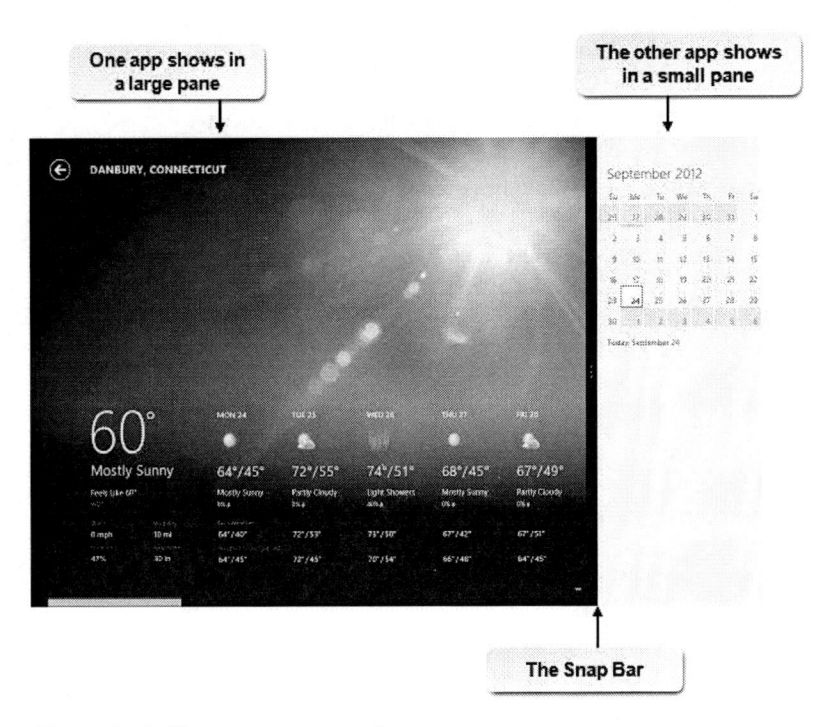

Figure 2-5: Two apps snapped.

The Close App Function

Because Windows 8 suspends apps when they are not in use and will close them automatically, you don't need to close an app when you're finished with it. However, having too many apps open at once can make switching between apps cumbersome, so it may make working easier to close any apps that you no longer need. There are two ways to close an app. You can move your pointer to the top of the screen and "drag" the app off the bottom of the screen, or you can use the Switcher to view the app tile, right-click on it and select Close.

	Access the Checklist tile on your LogicalCHOICE course screen for reference information and job aids on How to Multitask with Apps

ACTIVITY 2-3
Working with Multiple Apps

Before You Begin
The Weather app is active, but suspended. You are viewing the Start screen.

Scenario
Your company has another event in Boston after the Danbury race, and you may schedule post-race events there if weather permits. You can work with both apps at the same time, to check weather and schedule the days on your calendar. You will open the Calendar app and use the Snap feature to view both apps at once. When you're finished with the Weather app, you'll put the Calendar back on full screen.

1. Open the Calendar app.
    a) Select the **Calendar** tile to open the app.

    > **Note:** The calendar is laid out so you can see the whole month. Spaces for each day are large enough to show appointments, and the current day is highlighted in dark gray.

2. Snap the Calendar app.
    a) Move your pointer to the top of the Calendar page until it looks like a hand.
    b) Drag the Calendar to the right of the screen.
    c) When the snap bar appears, let go. The Calendar app snaps to the right pane.

3. Use the **Switcher** to access the Weather app and snap it.
    a) Move your pointer to the upper-left corner of the screen until the **Switcher** tile appears. It will look like the Weather app.
    b) Select the tile to activate the Weather app.

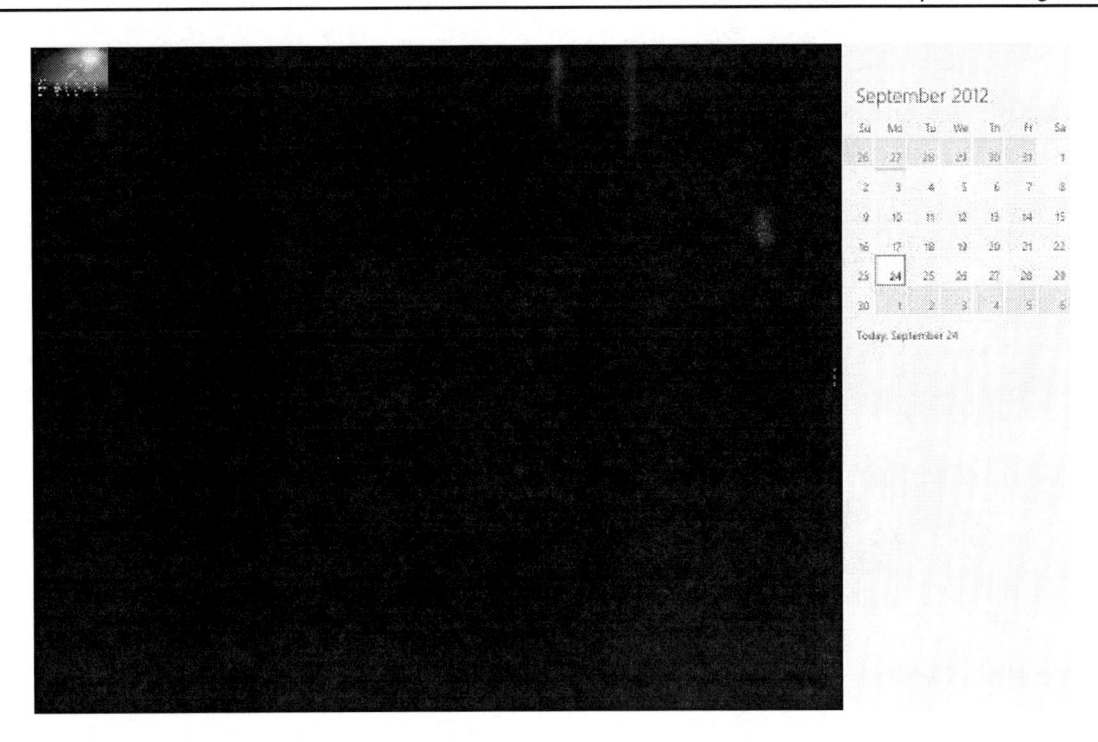

c) The Weather app snaps into the larger pane on the left side of the screen.

4. Search for a location in Weather.
   a) Using the **Search Charm,** search for *Boston*
   b) Above the **Search** text box, verify that Weather is the app indicated.

   c) Select **Boston, Massachusetts, United States.**
   d) Observe that the Weather app now shows weather for Boston, MA.
   e) Select anywhere on Weather to hide the command bar and close the **Search** pane.
   f) If necessary, use the scroll bar arrows at the bottom of Weather to view more of the screen so you can scroll through the weather for upcoming days.

5. Add events to the Calendar.
   a) Right-click the Calendar.
   b) Notice that two icons appear at the bottom of the **Calendar** screen: **Today** and **New.**
   c) Select the **New** icon.
   d) In the **What** text box, type *Boston race*

What

Boston race

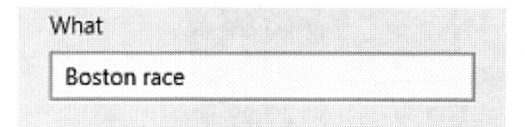

e) In the **When** box, change the day to next Sunday.
f) Select the **How long** box to open the menu.
g) From the **How long** menu, select **Custom**. New options appear.

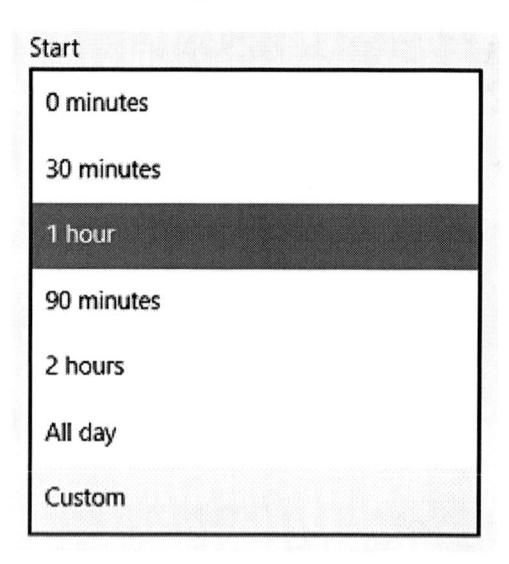

Start

0 minutes

30 minutes

1 hour

90 minutes

2 hours

All day

Custom

h) Below the **Start date**, check the **All day** check box. The **Start** and **End** times gray out.

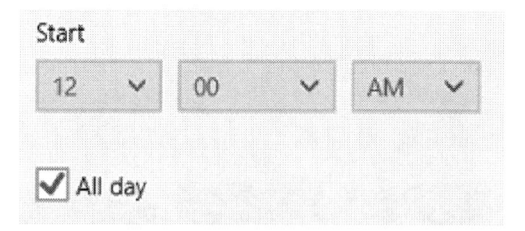

Start

12   00   AM

☑ All day

i) In the **Day** list, select the following Wednesday.

> **Note:** The list will only show the days for the current month. You may have to advance the Month if the following Wednesday is in the next month.

j) Save the event.

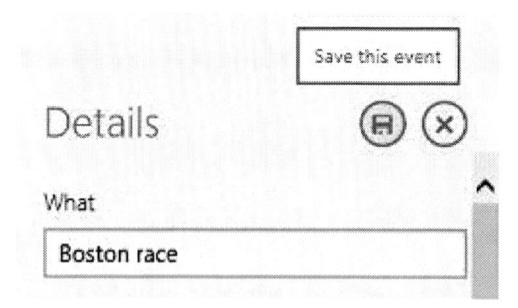

Save this event

Details

What

Boston race

k) Verify that there is now a gray line over the four days of your new event.

5	6	7	8	9
12	13	14	15	16
19	20	21	22	23

6. Change the snap proportions.
    a) Move your pointer over the snap bar and drag the bar to the left until the Weather app snaps into the smaller section and the Calendar app snaps into the larger section.
    b) Examine the calendar and confirm that your Boston Race event is displayed across the designated days.

7. Return Calendar to full-screen mode.
    a) Move your pointer over the snap bar and drag the bar off to the left of the screen. The Weather app disappears and is suspended.
    b) Verify that Calendar covers the entire screen and your Boston Race appointment spans the calendar from Sunday to Wednesday.

8. Access the **Switcher** to view open apps.
    a) Return to the **Start** screen.
    b) On the **Start** screen, move your pointer to the upper-left corner of the screen and slide it down the left side. All the open apps are displayed. In this case, you have the Calendar and Weather apps open. You can use these tiles to access any open app.
    c) Move your pointer away from the open apps pane to close it.

Summary

In this lesson, you used the Start screen to open an app, navigated around and entered text in an app, used the Search Charm, and worked with two apps at once using Snap and the Switcher. With these tools, you'll be able to open and work with the various apps you'll need.

Do you think that being able to use two apps at once will help you in your job? How might you use this feature?

Has your opinion of Windows 8 changed since Lesson 1? Is it easier than you thought?

> **Note:** Check your LogicalCHOICE Course screen for opportunities to interact with your classmates, peers, and the larger LogicalCHOICE online community about the topics covered in this course or other topics you are interested in. From the Course screen you can also access available resources for a more continuous learning experience.

http://www.lo-choice.com

3 | Working with Desktop Applications

Lesson Time: 1 hour, 30 minutes

Lesson Objectives

In this lesson, you will:

- Identify the elements of a Desktop window.

- Manage files and folders.

- Identify elements of a Desktop window.

- Use a Desktop application to create a file.

Lesson Introduction

Now that you've worked with two Microsoft® Windows® 8 Modern apps, Calendar and Weather, let's take a look at the Desktop and work with some classic applications. Because the Windows 8 Modern User Interface is so new, most of the applications you will be using will still be run on the classic Desktop environment. Becoming familiar with the Desktop and classic applications is essential to using a PC in your day-to-day work. This lesson introduces some of the basic concepts of the Desktop, files, and folders, and explores the navigation features common to Desktop applications. With this knowledge, you will be able to create and modify documents and keep your work on the PC organized.

TOPIC A

Navigate the Desktop

The Desktop makes use of icons and menus to aid in running and managing programs and files. In this topic, you'll take a look at the various components of the Desktop environment and how they can be used. Let's get started with a look at the Desktop!

The Desktop

In a typical office, two main components facilitate work: the filing cabinet and the desktop. You store and organize things in your filing cabinets, and do your work on your desktop. In earlier, or "classic," Windows operating system versions, the Desktop was the central place on your computer where you did your work. When you opened a program or a file, it would run on the Desktop. You may have a lot of things on your desk at work, but your desktop is still there, underneath. So it is with the Desktop on your PC. In Windows 8, the **Start** screen is the central place from which you open programs on your computer. However, because there are so many applications that still run only in the classic Desktop environment, Windows 8 provides the *Desktop* operating system as an app.

> **Note:** The background picture on the Desktop is called wallpaper, which you can change. Customizing the Desktop will be discussed later in the course.

Figure 3-1: The Desktop.

The Taskbar

The *taskbar* runs along the bottom of the screen and, like the **Start** screen, it can have common applications pinned to it for easier access. The taskbar has several functions; one of which is to display icons for those applications that are currently running. Selecting these icons enables you to switch back and forth between the open applications. Some applications allow you to have multiple files open. When this happens, you will see what looks like overlapping application icons on the taskbar. Select this multi-icon to view, switch to, or close the files that are open using that application. The taskbar also displays Internet access and signal strength, whether speakers are enabled, and notifications for software updates and system problems, among other things. While the default placement is along the bottom of the screen, you can move the taskbar to any edge of the screen, or set it to hide when not in use.

The Notification Area

The *Notification area* is located on the right side of the taskbar. This area displays icons for system functions, and each icon enables you to execute a different type of system command, such as safely removing external memory storage devices, connecting to the Internet and determining signal strength, receiving notification of issues with your computer or software updates, managing speaker volume, and more. This area is customizable, so you can add or remove icons and adjust the notification behaviors of each.

Tooltips

Just as with Modern apps, if you place your pointer over an icon or menu choice on the Desktop or in an application, a tooltip will appear. Tooltips display the application name or a brief description of what that application or menu choice will do.

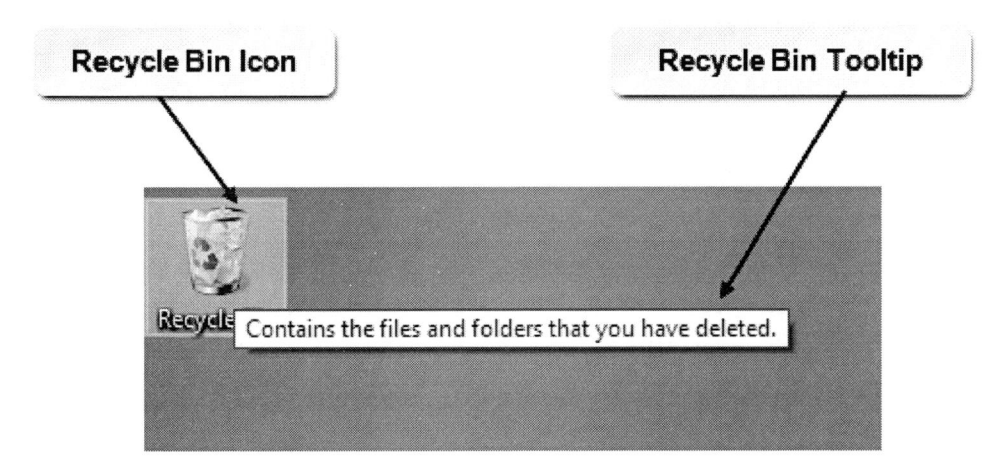

Figure 3-2: The tooltip for the Recycle Bin.

Context Menus

Context menus, also called jump lists, provide quick access to common tasks associated with different applications. When you right-click an application icon, the taskbar, or the Desktop itself, a context menu will display files frequently used or recently accessed by the application, and tasks that can be performed with that application. Some examples of tasks found on context menus include opening the application, opening the application to view a file listed on the context menu, and pinning or unpinning the application from the taskbar or Start screen. Some context menus show *keyboard shortcuts* associated with the tasks displayed. Keyboard shortcuts are keys or a combination of keys which, when pressed together or in succession, will execute a command that is otherwise executed by opening a menu or using a pointer. Keyboard shortcuts can increase efficiency by reducing the need to lift your hands from the keyboard in order to use the mouse to execute a command. Although not all of them will apply to Windows 8, you can find a complete list of keyboard shortcuts for Windows on the Microsoft Windows online site at **http://support.microsoft.com/kb/126449**.

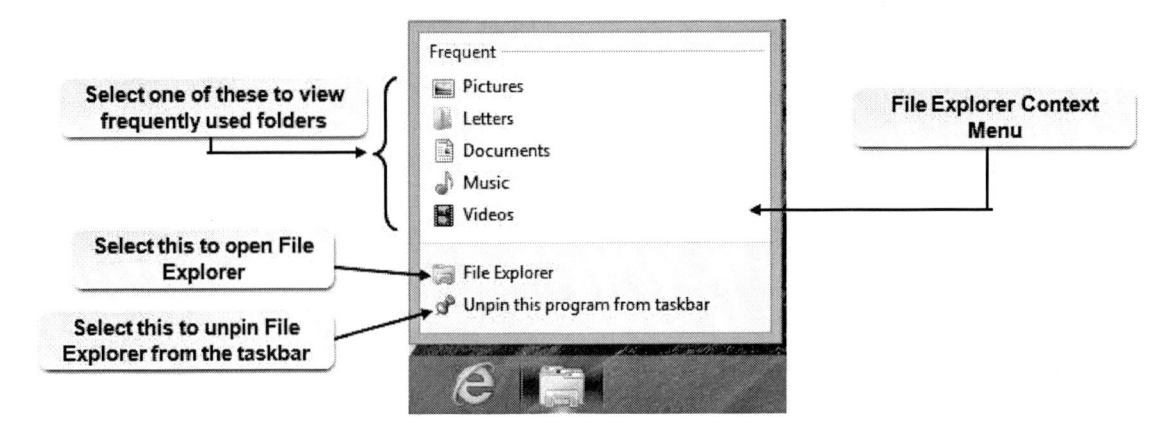

Figure 3-3: A context menu.

Application Icons

Application icons are small, labeled pictures that are displayed on the body of the Desktop. Like tiles on the **Start** screen, application icons act as shortcuts for running programs. Each icon has a stylized picture, along with the name of the application it's associated with. Unlike tiles, which you activate by clicking them once, application icons are activated when you double-click them. You can make application icons smaller or larger, and move and rearrange them to suit your needs. Application icon management options are available in the icon or Desktop context menus.

> **Note:** When Windows 8 is first loaded on your computer, one application icon, Recycle Bin, is displayed on the Desktop. The next topic has details about the Recycle Bin.

> Access the Checklist tile on your LogicalCHOICE course screen for reference information and job aids on How to Navigate the Desktop

ACTIVITY 3-1
Navigating the Desktop

Before You Begin
You are at the Start screen and the open apps display bar is closed.

Scenario
Because you'll be using the Desktop often, you want to examine its basic elements: the Notification area, program icons, and the taskbar. Since the Notification area gives you control over system status notifications, external storage management, and common program features, you'll examine the icons in that area and access icon menus. You'll also open a context menu and examine some of the available options. And finally, you're not sure if you like having the taskbar on the bottom of the screen, so you'll experiment with it in different positions, and hide it.

---

1. Open the Desktop.
    a) On the **Start** screen, select the **Desktop** tile.
    b) Verify that the Desktop opens.

2. Identify elements of the Desktop.
    a) Locate the application icon on the Desktop.

    b) Locate the taskbar along the bottom of the page.

3. Locate the application icons pinned to the taskbar and view their tooltips.
    a) Place your pointer over the icons to view their tooltip descriptions. The tooltips show the application names: Internet Explorer and File Explorer.

4. Locate the icons in the **Notification** area and view their tooltips.
    a) Place your pointer over the **Notification** icons to view their tooltips.

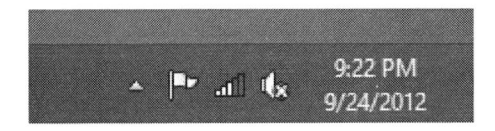

5. Access the **Action Center**.
    a) In the **Notification** area, select the **Action Center** icon. The **Action Center** menu opens.
    b) Read the **Access Center** description.
    c) Select anywhere on the Desktop background to close the **Action Center** menu.

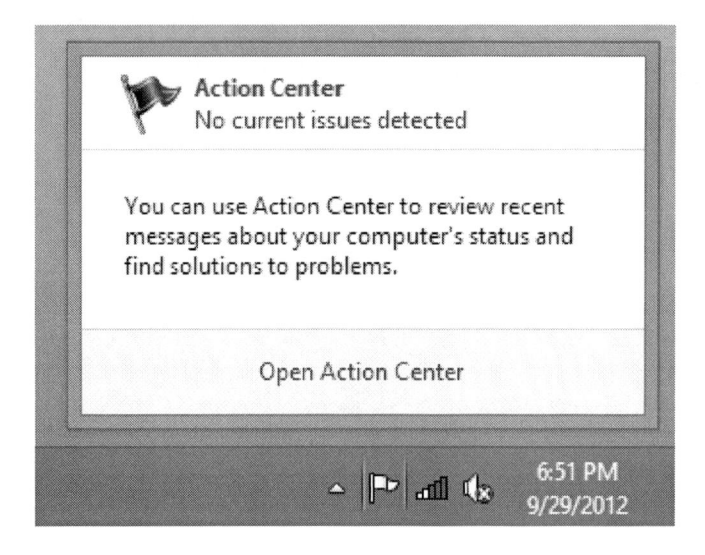

6. Access the **Action Center** context menu.
   a) Right-click the **Action Center** icon. The **Action Center** context menu opens.
   b) Review the options available.
   c) Select anywhere on the Desktop background to close the **Action Center** context menu.

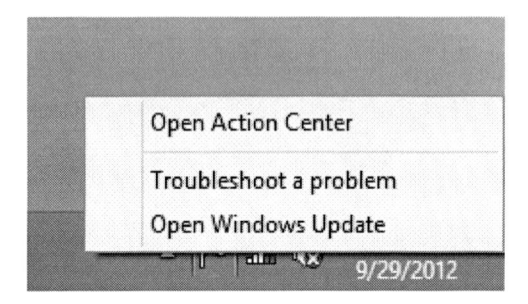

7. Access the hidden icons.
   a) If available, select the **Show Hidden Icons** up arrow.
   b) Drag the **Action Center** icon up into the **Hidden Icons** menu.

   > Note: If the **Show Hidden Icons** up arrow is not present, dragging an icon up from the taskbar will open the **Hidden Icons** menu.

   c) Verify that the **Action Center** icon is no longer on the taskbar, but is now included in the **Hidden Icons** menu.
   d) Drag the **Action Center** icon back to the taskbar.
   e) Select anywhere outside of the **Show Hidden Icons** menu to close it.

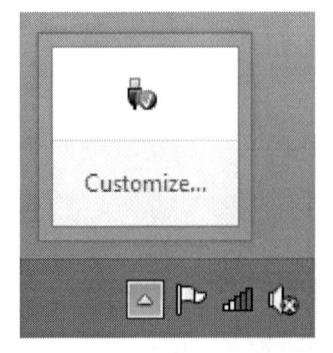

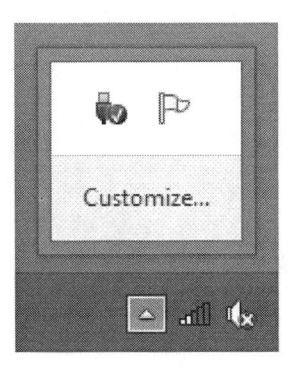

8. Display the taskbar in alternate locations.
   a) Right-click the taskbar to open the taskbar context menu.
   b) Verify that **Lock the taskbar** is checked.

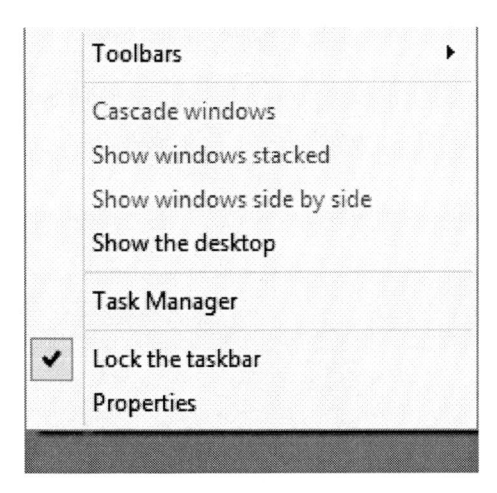

   c) Select **Lock the taskbar** to uncheck this option. The context menu closes.
   d) Open the taskbar context menu.
   e) Verify that **Lock the taskbar** is no longer checked.
   f) Select outside of the context menu to close it.
   g) Drag the taskbar diagonally to the left and release. The taskbar is now displayed on the left edge of the screen.
   h) Drag the taskbar diagonally and to the top of the screen and release. The taskbar is now across the top edge of the screen.
   i) Drag the taskbar back to the bottom.
   j) Open the taskbar context menu and select **Lock the taskbar** to lock it.

   > **Note:** The taskbar can be moved and locked to any side you choose.

9. Access taskbar properties.
   a) Open the taskbar context menu.
   b) Select **Properties.** Verify that the taskbar **Properties** menu opens.
   c) Select **Auto-hide the taskbar** to check it.
   d) Select **Apply.** Verify that the taskbar slides down and becomes hidden.
   e) Move your mouse off the bottom of the screen. Confirm that the taskbar reappears.
   f) Select **OK** to confirm this change and close the menu.

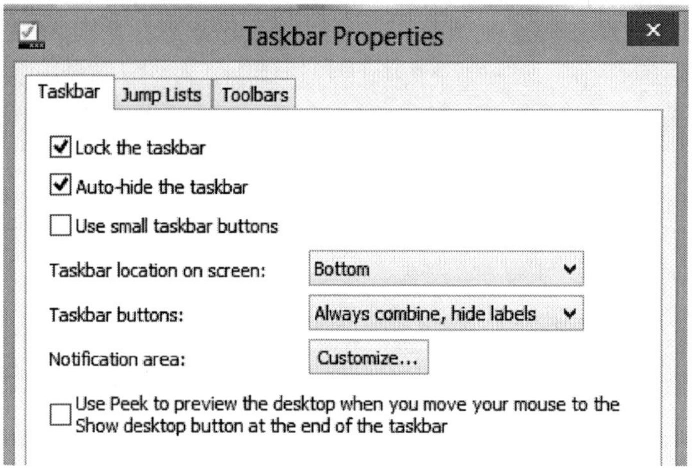
Taskbar Properties
Taskbar
Jump Lists
Toolbars
Lock the taskbar
Auto-hide the taskbar
Use small taskbar buttons
Taskbar location on screen:
Bottom
Taskbar buttons:
Always combine, hide labels
Notification area:
Customize...
Use Peek to preview the desktop when you move your mouse to the Show desktop button at the end of the taskbar

TOPIC B

Manage Files and Folders with File Explorer

Now that you've become familiar with some of the elements of the Desktop, it's time to take a look at the organization and management of the products of your work: files and folders. Just as it is with paper files and folders, it's difficult to work on the computer if there's no organization. In this topic, you will explore how data is stored on your PC and how you can manage your files using the methods available on the Desktop.

Files and Folders

In your office, you work with paper files that you store within labeled folders in a file cabinet. If the files and folders are properly labeled and organized, it's easy to find what you're looking for. Computers work in a similar fashion, where the documents, reports, and other data you create in your applications are saved in files and stored in folders. When you are ready to save your work in an application, you assign a name to the file and select or create a folder in which to store it. The name you give to the file should be descriptive enough to help you find the file in the future.

Folders are the directories in which you store your files. As with a file cabinet, you can have folders within folders. For instance, on your computer, you might have a folder for all invoices for the current year. That might be the equivalent of a cabinet drawer. Within that, you might have a folder for each customer, labeled with the customer or company name. Within the customer folder would be all of the invoices, or files, for that customer. In this way, folders keep your files organized for easy access.

Libraries

Libraries look and act like folders, but are designed to be more like the card catalog. They don't actually store your files; instead, they keep track of file and folder locations so you don't have to, and present them in a single area. Libraries can even keep track of folders that are stored on different hard drives, removable storage (flash drive or SD card), or even a different computer. Windows comes preloaded with four libraries: **Documents, Music, Pictures,** and **Videos.** Each library is further divided into two categories: your files and public files. Windows 8 provides the connectivity between programs and the libraries, so that word-processor program data files are displayed in the **Documents** library, picture files are displayed in the **Photos** library, and so on. You can create new libraries if these four don't meet your needs.

File Explorer

Just like with a file cabinet, the files and folders on your PC occasionally need to be cleaned up and reorganized. *File Explorer* gives you a way of viewing and managing the filing system on your computer. Using File Explorer, you can rename, move, or copy any file or folder, as well as create new folders. You can even open files to work on. When you open a file from within File Explorer, the appropriate application is started and your file is opened within the application.

File Explorer runs in a directory window, which displays files, folders, and subfolders and contains several elements that are common to Desktop windows.

Element	Function
Navigation pane	Shows you locations available on your computer (libraries, favorite or recently used locations, and storage drives), as well as other computers that may be networked to yours.

Element	Function
Contents pane	Displays the files and folders contained within the locations listed in the navigation pane.
Tabs	Categories of tools used for managing your files. Each tab has an attached ribbon or menu of specialized tools. The tabs vary depending on the application in which they appear, but most applications have **File** and **Home** tabs.
Ribbon	A menu of file-management tools related to the tab selected. The tools contained within the ribbon vary depending on the application in which they appear.
Address bar	The **Address** bar shows you what folder you are in and the structure of the path from the file or folder up to the library or disk-drive level. You can select any of these levels to move up the structure.
Search bar	The **Search** bar allows you to search for files and folders within disk drives, libraries, and folders.
Back and **Forward** buttons	Use these to go to a previous page, or forward a page, respectively.
Up a Level button	Use this button to move up a level within the file path structure.
Caret	Indicates that a library or folder contains subfolders. You select the caret to open the library or folder and display its contents, or to close the library or folder and hide the contents.

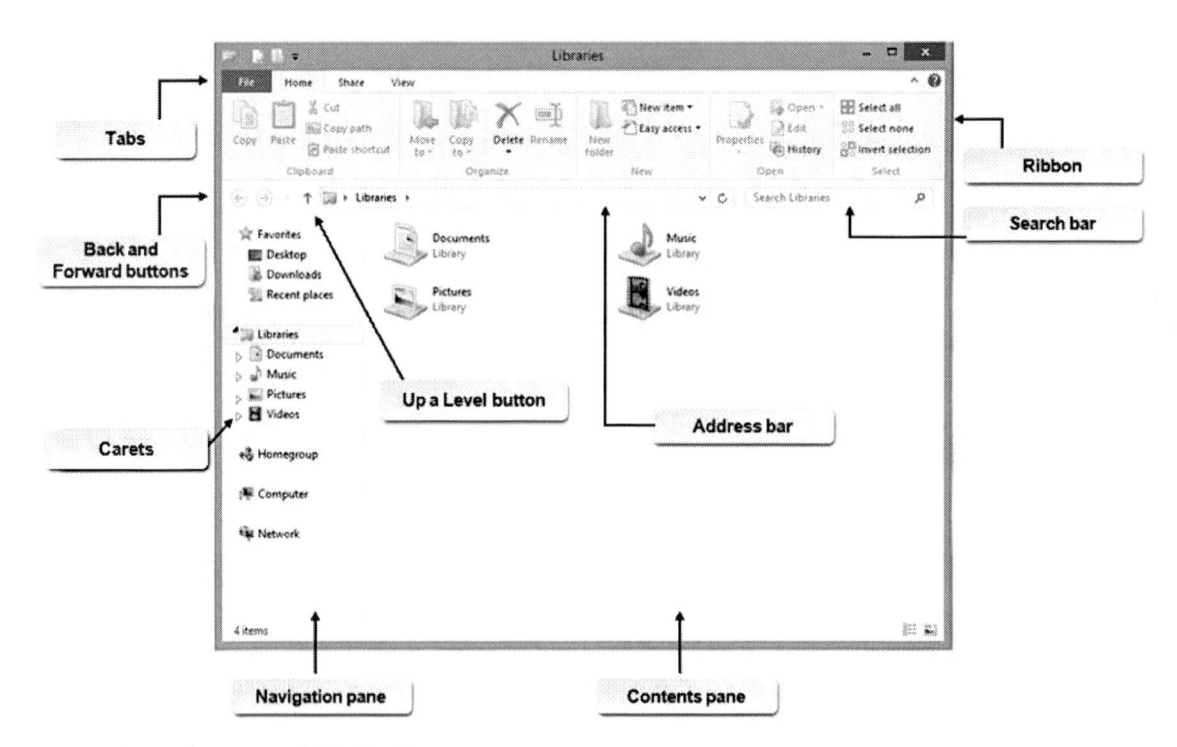

Figure 3-4: Elements of File Explorer.

Tabs and the Ribbon

The *ribbon* comprises tabs, groups, and commands for managing, editing, and viewing files. You can select each of the tabs along the top of the ribbon to access a specialized ribbon of tools related to that tab. Access functions on the ribbon by selecting the icons on the ribbon. Some icons will open drop-down menus or dialog boxes offering more options. Tabs and the contents of ribbons vary from application to application, although most have **File** and **Home** tabs. Some smaller applications, such as the Calculator, don't have a ribbon, but rely on tabs that display drop-down menus. You can expand or minimize the ribbon by using the caret at the right end of the **Tabs** bar.

The Recycle Bin

When you delete something from your computer, such as a data file or folder, Windows doesn't actually delete it, but moves it into the *Recycle Bin*. The file will remain in the Recycle Bin until you empty it, at which time all files in the Recycle Bin will be permanently deleted. You can go into the Recycle Bin and delete files individually, restore a file that was deleted, or empty the Recycle Bin. To access the Recycle bin, double-click the **Recycle Bin** program icon. If you look on the taskbar, you'll note that the Recycle Bin uses the File Explorer directory window in which to run. If you run both the Recycle Bin and File Explorer at the same time, the taskbar will show the overlapping File Explorer icon. The Recycle Bin application icon changes as it fills up with deleted files. When it is empty, the basket icon looks empty. As it fills up, more "paper" appears in the basket.

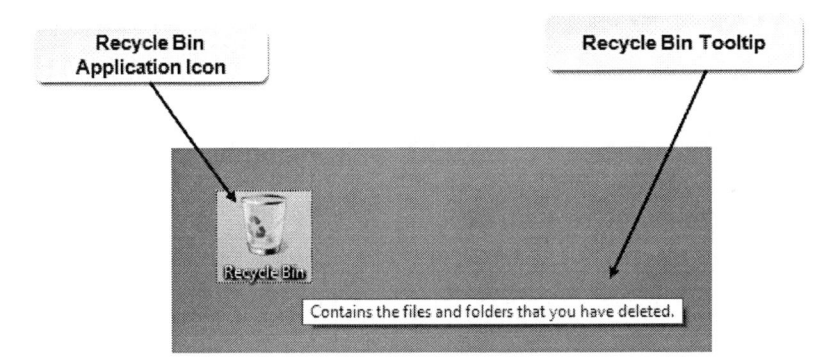

Figure 3-5: The Recycle Bin icon and tooltip.

Dialog Boxes

A dialog box is a type of window that pops up, usually from within an application, and offers several options or instructions, prompting the user to respond. They are called dialog boxes because of this interaction or "dialog" between the computer and the user.

> Access the Checklist tile on your LogicalCHOICE course screen for reference information and job aids on How to Manage Files and Folders

ACTIVITY 3-2
Managing Files and Folders

Data Files
C:\091102Data\Working with Desktop Applications\Tents.rtf

Scenario
You've had some experience exploring Windows 8. To increase your efficiency and reduce any frustration, you want to make sure you can manage your files at work and keep them organized. You will to familiarize yourself with File Explorer, the Desktop file management application. Also, you decide to practice working with libraries, folders, and files. As you will do many times in your work, you'll create and name a new folder and copy and move a file into that folder. You'll also delete a file and open the Recycle Bin to permanently remove the file from your PC.

1. Open File Explorer.
    a) On the taskbar, select the **File Explorer** icon.

    b) Verify that File Explorer is open.

2. Access the ribbon and tabs.
    a) Select the **Home** tab. The **Home** ribbon displays.

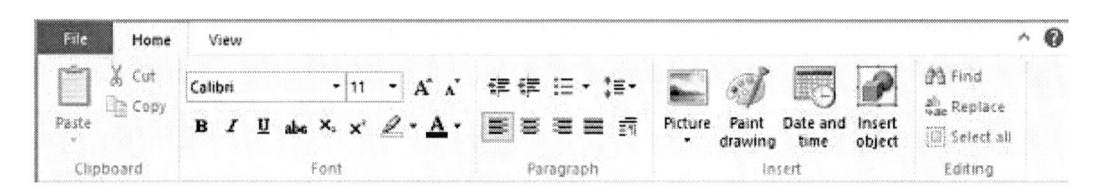

    > **Note:** If necessary, use the ribbon caret to open the ribbon.

    b) Identify the commands within the groups on the **Home** ribbon.
    c) Select the **File** tab. This tab displays its tools in a menu.
    d) Observe that some of the menu choices have a caret next to them. This indicates that there are submenus for that menu option.
    e) Place your pointer over the carets to view the commands in the submenus.

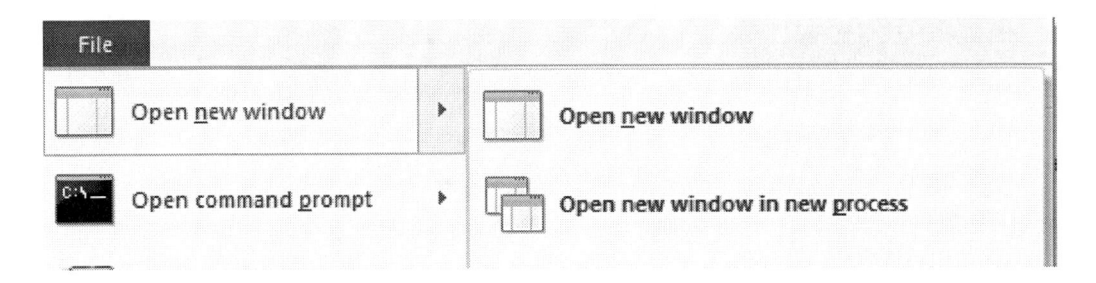

File	
Open new window ▶	Open new window
Open command prompt ▶	Open new window in new process

   f) Select the **File** tab to close the menu.
   g) Verify that the **Home** ribbon is active.

3. View the contents of libraries and folders.
   a) In the **Navigation** pane, select the **Documents** library caret to view the folders contained within it.
   b) Verify there are two folders: **My Documents** and **Public Documents**.
   c) Select **My Documents** to view the contents of the folder.

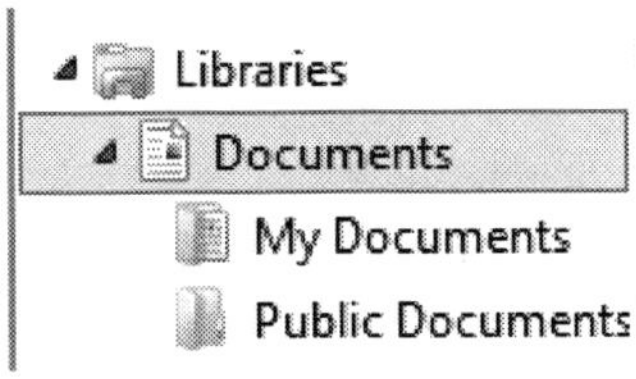

   ▲ Libraries
     ▲ Documents
        My Documents
        Public Documents

   d) In the **Contents** pane, verify that the file **Tents** is displayed.

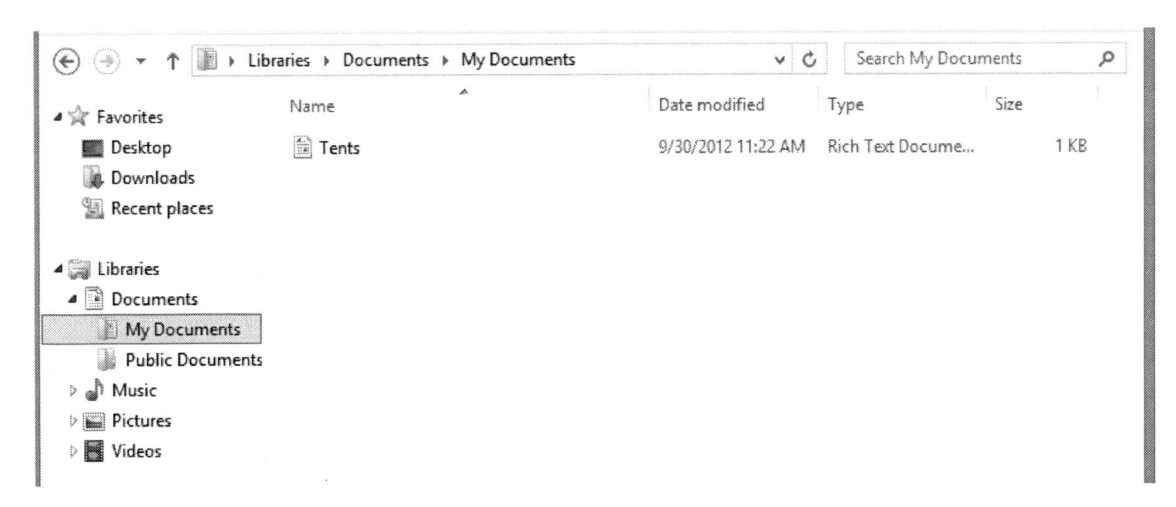

Name	Date modified	Type	Size
Tents	9/30/2012 11:22 AM	Rich Text Docume...	1 KB

   ▲ ☆ Favorites
      Desktop
      Downloads
      Recent places

   ▲ Libraries
      ▲ Documents
         My Documents
         Public Documents
      ▷ Music
      ▷ Pictures
      ▷ Videos

4. Create and name a new folder.
   a) On the **Home** tab ribbon, select **New Folder**.

   > **Note:** If necessary, select the ribbon caret to open the ribbon.

b) In the **File name** text box, type *Letters* to name the folder.
c) Press the **Enter** key.

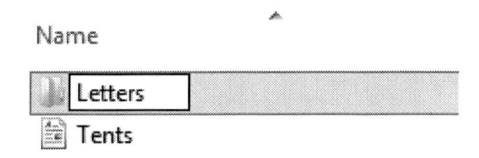

d) Verify that the folder **Letters** is now a subfolder within **My Documents**.
e) Double-click the **Letters** folder to open it. Confirm it is an empty folder.

5. Copy a file.
    a) Select the **Up a Level** arrow to return to **My Documents** and select the file **Tents**.
    b) On the ribbon, select **Copy to**.

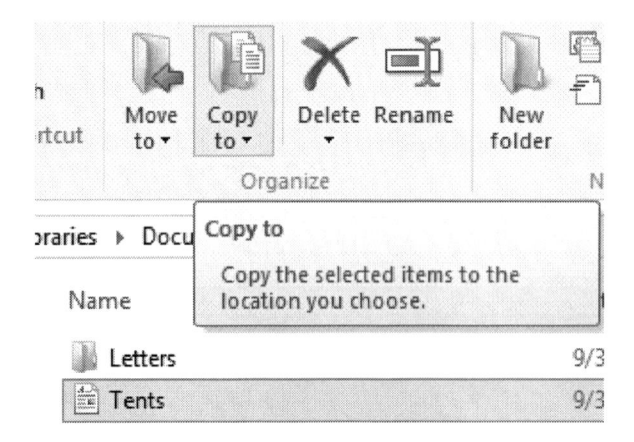

    c) From the list, select **Choose location.**

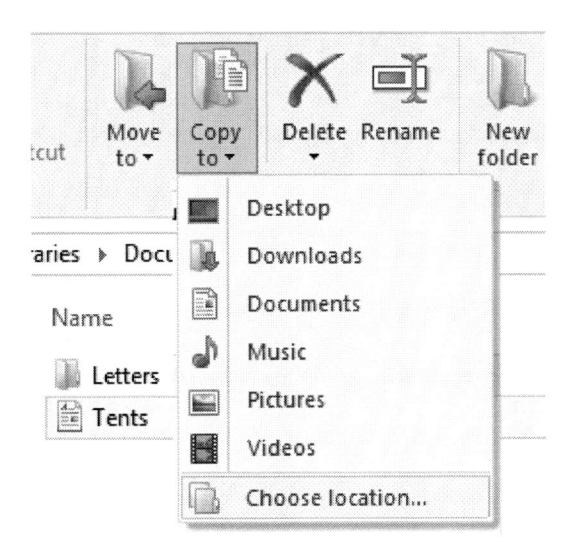

d) In the dialog box, select the **Libraries** caret to view its subfolders.
e) In the dialog box, select the **Documents** caret to view its subfolders.
f) In the dialog box, select the **My Documents** caret to view its subfolders.
g) In the dialog box, select the **Letters** folder.

h) Select **Copy.**
i) Verify that **My Documents** still contains the folder **Letters** and the file **Tents.**
j) Double-click the **Letters** folder to open it.
k) Confirm that a copy of the file **Tents** is contained there. There are now two copies of **Tents.**

6. Delete a file.
   a) In the **Letters** folder, select the file **Tents.**
   b) On the ribbon, select **Delete.**
   c) Confirm that the file is deleted and no longer resides in the **Letters** folder.

d) View the contents of **My Documents.** Confirm that the original file **Tents** is still there.

7. Move a file.
    a) Drag the file **Tents** up into the **Letters** folder. When **Letters** is highlighted, release the file.

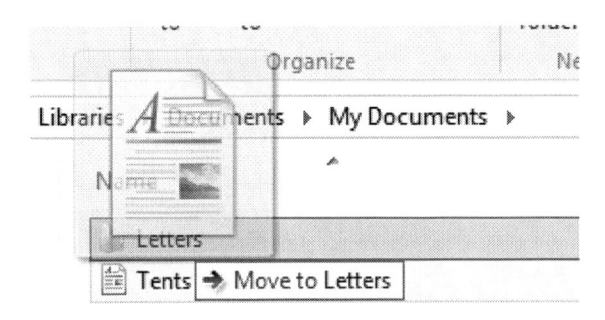

    b) Verify that the file **Tents** is no longer listed in the **My Documents** folder.
    c) Open the **Letters** folder.
    d) Confirm that the file **Tents** has been moved to the **Letter s** folder.

8. View the contents of the Recycle Bin and then empty the Recycle Bin.
    a) Double-click the **Recycle Bin** application icon on the **Desktop** to open the Recycle Bin.
    b) Verify that the application opens.

    > **Note:** Recycle Bin uses the File Explorer directory window. Because both File Explorer and the Recycle bin are open, there are two File Explorer icons overlapping on the taskbar.

    c) Select the **Home** tab.
    d) Identify the groups on the **Home** ribbon.
    e) Identify the commands on the **Home** ribbon. You used some of these commands in File Explorer.

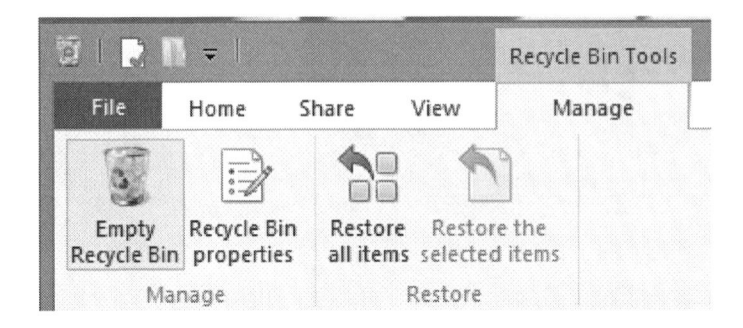

    f) Select the **Manage** tab to return to **Recycle Bin Tools**.
    g) Identify the commands on the ribbon. You can empty the Recycle Bin, or restore items.
    h) In the **Contents** pane, observe that the file that you deleted, the copy of **Tents**, is displayed.
    i) Select **Empty Recycle Bin.**

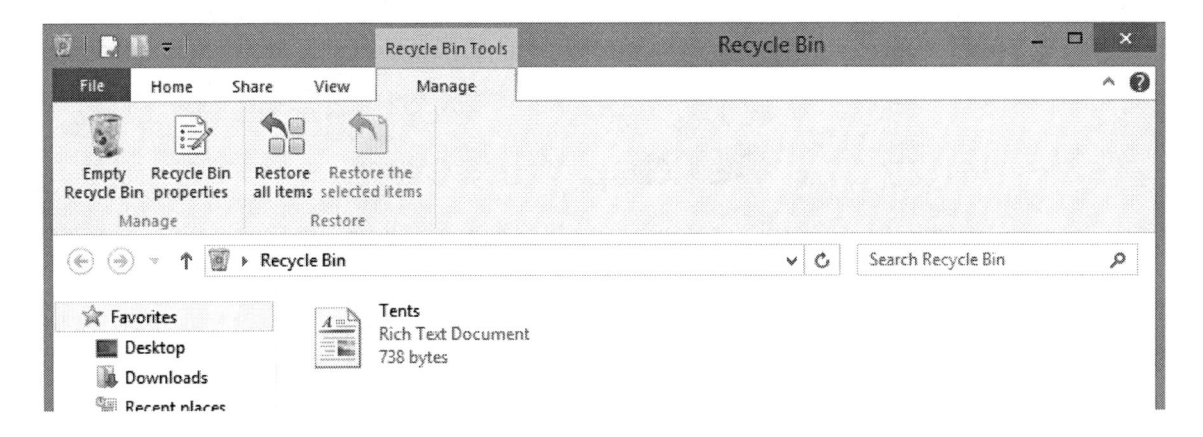

j) In the **Delete File** dialog box, select **Yes**. The file is deleted and no longer appears in the **Contents** pane.

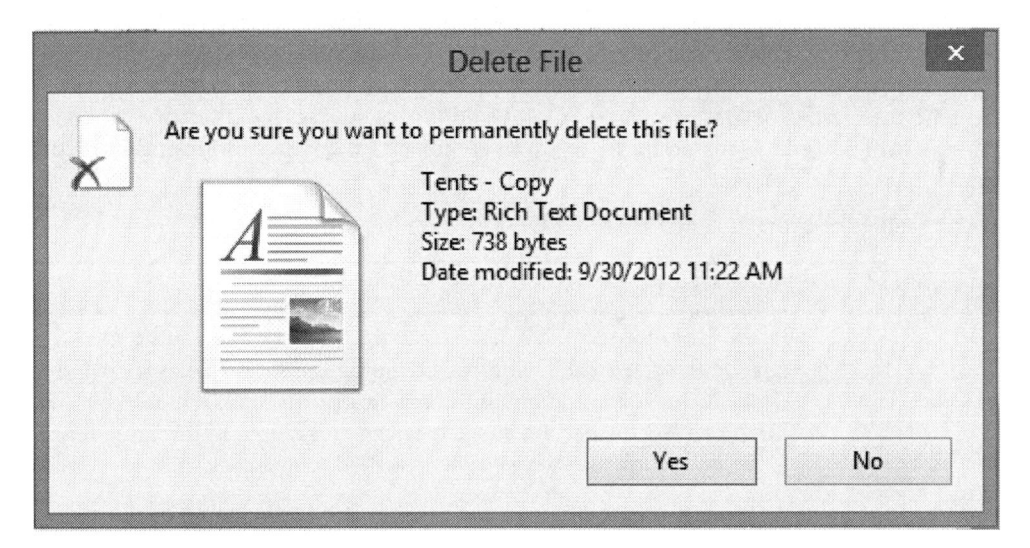

Note: To further explore File Explorer navigation techniques, you can access the LearnTO **Customize File Explorer** presentation from the **LearnTO** tile on the LogicalCHOICE Course screen.

TOPIC C

Elements of a Desktop Window

As you saw with the File Explorer and Recycle Bin windows, all Desktop applications are designed to run within a standardized window using common elements. Once you learn how the components of a window work, learning new applications and switching between applications will be easier. In this topic, you'll identify more elements of a Desktop window and learn how to move, resize, and switch between windows.

Desktop Windows

When you run an application on the Desktop, it runs within a graphical window, with borders that you can drag to resize and change the shape of the window. Although you can have multiple windows open, only one window can be active at a time. To make it easy to identify the active window, the borders of the active window are colorful, while the borders of inactive windows are gray. There are three types of Desktop windows covered in this course: the directory window and the dialog box (which were discussed in the previous topic), and the application window, explored in this topic.

The following table describes the elements of a Desktop window.

Window Element	Description
Border	In the **Restore** state, borders frame the window and can be used to change the size of the window. Dragging the sides makes the window wider or narrower; dragging the top or bottom makes it taller or shorter. Dragging a corner will adjust the width and height at the same time. An exception to this is the dialog box, which typically cannot be resized.
Title bar	At the top of the window, the title bar shows the name of the application or file you are using. You can use the title bar to drag the window, and to snap the application, just as you snap Modern apps.
Minimize button	This button lets you temporarily close the window, leaving the application running. The application icon will remain on the taskbar and will be highlighted to indicate the application is still running.
Restore/Maximize button	These two share the same position on the title bar. The **Maximize** icon looks like a single window and the **Restore** icon looks like two windows cascading. **Maximize** resizes the window to fill the screen. No borders will be visible. **Restore** reduces the window to run in a smaller size, with visible borders. Most dialog boxes cannot be maximized.
Close button	Shuts down the application and closes the window.
Control menu	Gives you **Minimize, Maximize, Restore**, and **Close** options in menu form. May also have other options depending on the application.
Quick Access Toolbar	Provides icons for performing frequently used actions such as saving and printing. May also have other options depending on the application.
Status bar	The status bar is the area where the application displays information about items selected, what page you are on, if **Caps Lock** is on, and other messages that aid in use of the application. There is often a **Zoom** bar on the right side, which lets you increase or decrease the size of the page being viewed.

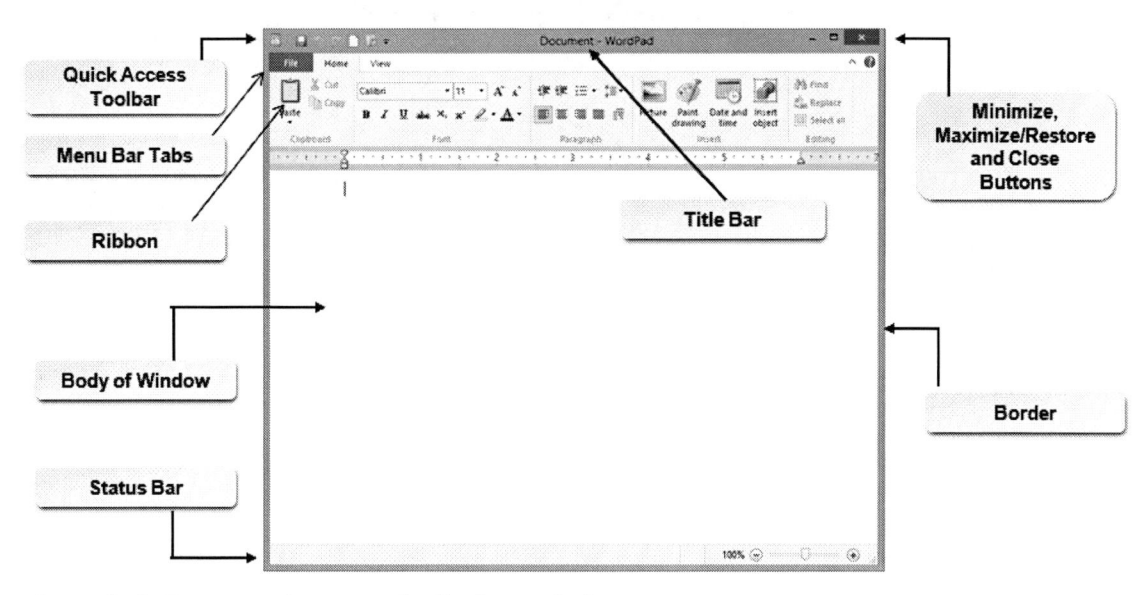

Figure 3-6: Common elements of a Desktop window.

The Quick Access Toolbar

The **Quick Access Toolbar** displays icons that, with one click, can perform functions that otherwise might take several motions. In applications such as word processors and spreadsheets, this tiny area can be a huge time saver. To add a function to the **Quick Access Toolbar,** select the **Customize Quick Access Toolbar** icon to open the menu and select the function to be included on the display. Functions that are already displayed on the toolbar have a check next to them. To remove a function from the toolbar, select the check to remove it.

The following table lists options that are commonly found on the **Quick Access Toolbar**.

Icon	Function
Open	Opens an existing file.
New	Opens a blank page so you can create a new file.
Save	Saves the file using the current name and location. You can use this function the first time you save a new file, but you will be directed to the **Save As** dialog box.
Save As	Requires you to assign a name and location to the file before saving it. Use this when you wish to keep both the original file and the modified file, and the first time you save a new file.
Undo	Undoes the last action taken on the file. Some applications allow you to undo several actions.
Redo	Repeats the last action taken on the file. Can be used to reverse the last **Undo.**
Print	Sends the file to a printer or a print file. This option allows you to select a printer, select the pages to be printed, and adjust settings on the printer before sending the file to be printed.
Print Preview	Allows you to view the file on the screen as it would look if it were printed on a piece of paper.
Quick Print	Allows you to print the file without having to select a printer or print options. It uses the same settings as the most recently printed file.

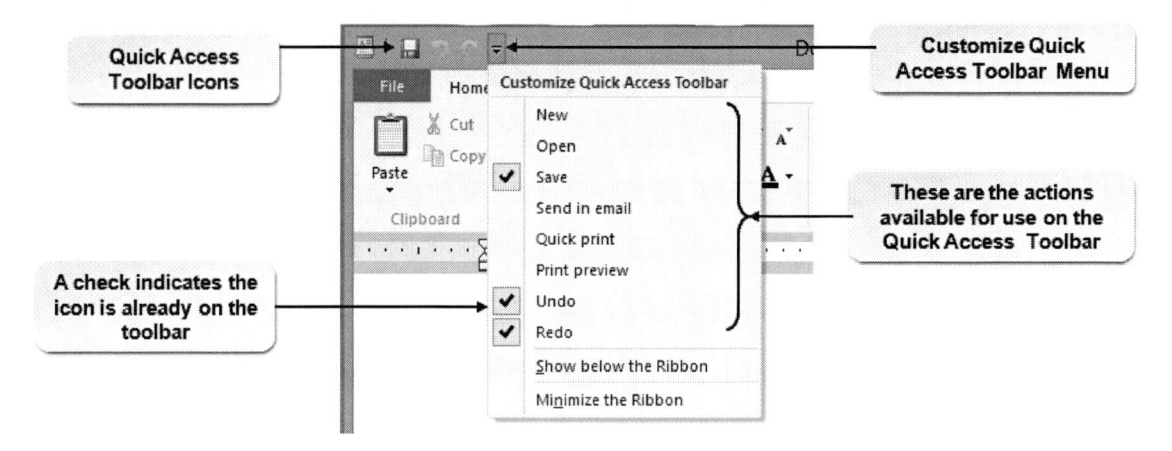

Figure 3-7: Typical Quick Access Toolbar menu customization options.

The Body of the Window

The *body* of the window is where your work is displayed. It takes on a different appearance depending on the application. In a directory window, the body comprises the **Navigation** pane and the **Contents** pane. In a word-processing application, the body of the window is where you type; it looks like a piece of paper with rulers along the top or left. In a spreadsheet, the body is a grid pattern composed of **rows** and **columns** of **cells** in which you do your work.

Snap, Cascade, Stack, and Switch Functions

Just like with apps, you can switch between windows, and snap them to view more than one at a time. Desktop windows can also be cascaded and stacked on top of each other, and you can have more than two windows showing at once. You can snap windows using the title bar to drag the window, but cascade and stack are only available by opening the taskbar context menu.

> Access the Checklist tile on your LogicalCHOICE course screen for reference information and job aids on How to Use the Elements of a Desktop Window

ACTIVITY 3-3
Working with the Elements of a Desktop Window

Data Files
C:\091102Data\Working with Desktop Applications\Tents.rtf

Before You Begin
File Explorer and the Recycle Bin are open and in the Restore state.

Scenario
Now that you know how to manage files and folders, and have worked with directory windows and dialog boxes, you want to focus on where the real work takes place on the Desktop: within application windows. To get used to multitasking on your PC, you'll familiarize yourself with opening and closing applications, and arranging windows on the screen. You also decide to customize the ribbon to add commands you plan on using often.

---

1. Close a window.
    a) On the title bar of the Recycle Bin window, locate the **Close** button.
    b) Select the **Close** button to close the Recycle Bin.
    c) Verify that the File Explorer window is now the active window.

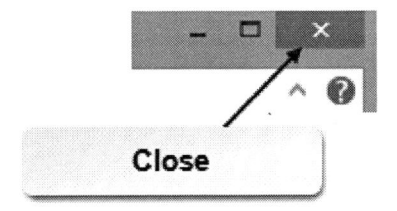

2. Move a window.
    a) Place your pointer on the File Explorer title bar and drag the window around on the page.
    b) Release the title bar. The window will stay where you put it.

    > **Caution:** The title bar has two move functions. For moving the window, the pointer should retain its normal shape. For resizing the border, the pointer should look like a two-headed arrow.

3. Resize a window.
    a) Place your pointer over the right border of the window. The pointer becomes a two-headed arrow.

    Vertical Resize

    Horizontal Resize

    b) Drag the border to the right. The window gets wider.

c) Place your pointer on the top edge of the title bar until it becomes a two-headed arrow.
d) Drag the top border up to make the window taller.

> **Note:** This resizing works on all of the window borders.

4. Maximize a window.
    a) On the title bar, locate the **Maximize** button.
    b) Select the **Maximize** button to enlarge the window. The window fills the screen, and you cannot see the window borders.

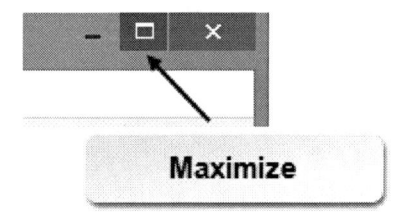

5. Minimize a window.
    a) Select the **Minimize** button. The window closes, but you can see on the taskbar that the **File Explorer** icon is highlighted, indicating that the application is still running.
    b) On the taskbar, select the **File Explorer** icon to maximize the window again.

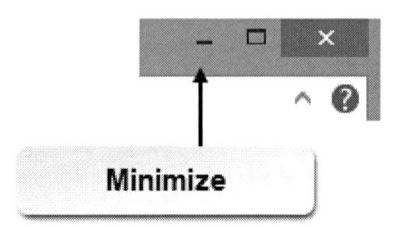

6. Snap a Desktop window.
    a) Using the title bar, drag the File Explorer window off the right side of the screen.
    b) When you see a small visual "wave" around your pointer, release the window. The window snaps to fill the right side of the screen.
    c) Verify that you can see the Desktop on the left side of your screen. 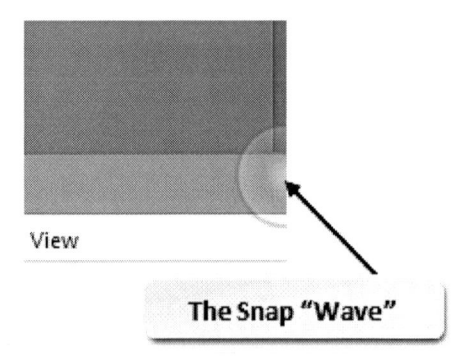

7. Open an application.
    a) Using the **Search Charm**, search for **WordPad**.
    b) From the search results, select **WordPad**.

c) On the Desktop, verify that File Explorer is still snapped, and WordPad is in the **Restore** state. WordPad is the active window.

8. Snap a window on the Desktop.
   a) Using the title bar, drag the WordPad window off the left side of the screen.
   b) Release the window when you see the small wave. You now have two applications displayed on the screen. WordPad is still the active window.

9. Cascade multiple windows.
   a) Right-click the taskbar to open the context menu. The menu has options for cascading, stacking, and snapping windows.
   b) Select **Cascade windows.** The windows cascade down from the upper-left corner.

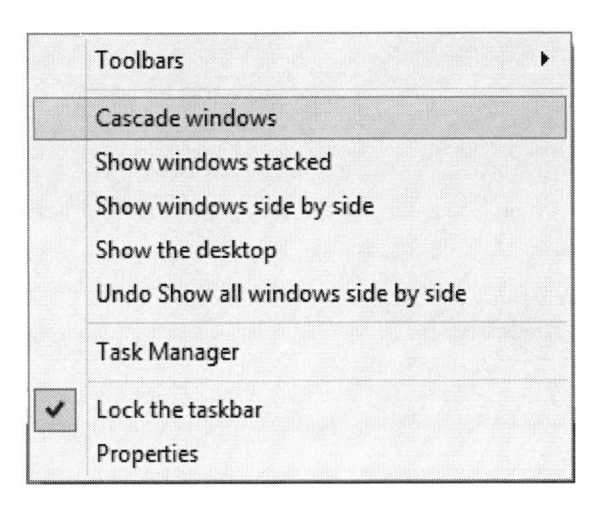

Toolbars ▶
Cascade windows
Show windows stacked
Show windows side by side
Show the desktop
Undo Show all windows side by side
Task Manager
✓ Lock the taskbar
Properties

10. Stack multiple windows.
    a) Open the context menu again and select **Show windows stacked.** The windows rearrange horizontally, with the active window on the top.

11. Arrange windows side by side.
    a) Open the context menu again and select **Show windows side by side.** The windows are put back in the snapped position.

12. Maximize a window.
    a) Close File Explorer.
    b) In the WordPad window, select the **Maximize** button to maximize WordPad.

13. Add icons to the WordPad **Quick Access Toolbar**.
    a) Select the **Customize Quick Access Toolbar** icon to open the menu. **Save, Undo,** and **Redo** are checked. They are already on the toolbar.

Customize Quick Access Toolbar menu showing options: New, Open, ✓ Save, Send in e-mail, Quick print, Print preview, ✓ Undo, ✓ Redo, Show below the Ribbon, Minimize the Ribbon.

    b) Select **New**.
    c) Verify that the **Quick Access Toolbar** now has an icon of a blank sheet of paper. This icon will open a new, blank document.

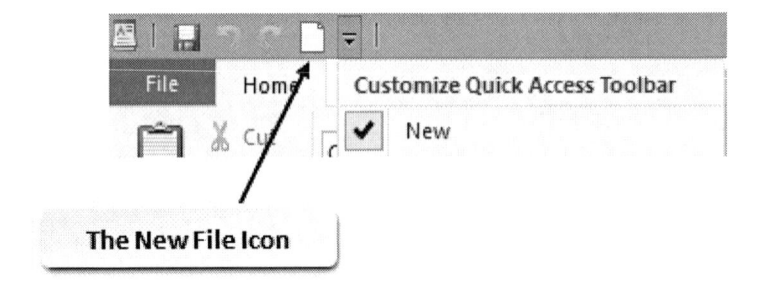

The New File Icon is shown on the Quick Access Toolbar, with New now checked in the Customize Quick Access Toolbar menu.

    d) Open the **Customize Quick Access Toolbar** again.
    e) Confirm that **New** now has a check next to it, signifying that it is available on the toolbar.
    f) From the menu, select **Open**.
    g) Verify that the toolbar now has an icon of a folder with an arrow pointing into it. This icon will open an existing document.

TOPIC D

Create and Modify Files with Desktop Applications

Windows 8 comes bundled with a few simple but useful applications. You've already used File Explorer and Recycle Bin, and have opened WordPad. WordPad is a simple word processor that you can use to create documents and get familiar with the functions and capabilities of a typical word processor.

New Documents

When you open an application, whether it is a word processor, spreadsheet, or graphics program, the work area is blank and ready for you to create a new document. However, there will be times when you are working on a document and wish to have a blank slate to create a new document. To do this, you can use the **File** menu and select **New.** If you have customized your **Quick Access Toolbar,** you can select the **New** icon and it will do the same thing. Some applications, such as WordPad and NotePad, will not let you have more than one document open at a time and will close the file you are currently working on when you open a second file. When this happens, the application will ask if you want to save your work on the current file before it is closed.

Open an Existing Document

It's often useful to be able to modify existing files. You may have a spreadsheet that needs correcting or updating; or you may find that reusing a document and making a few small changes can save time. From the **File** tab menu, when you select **Open** (or select the **Quick Access Toolbar's Open** icon), a dialog box will open, allowing you to search through your folders to find the file you wish to use. Select the file and select **Open,** and your file will be opened for use. You can make any changes you wish, but no changes will be permanent until you save the file with the changes.

Save

When you are finished working on a file, or you have reached a point at which you don't want to lose your work, you can save the file. When you make changes to an existing file, you can save it under the current name, which will overwrite the previous version of the file, or you can use **Save As** to give it a new name. This will give you a new file and will leave the original file as it was. The first time you save a new file, you will be asked to name it and choose a folder to save it in. File names can include letters, numbers, spaces, and some special characters. Names cannot contain the following symbols: < > : " / \ | ? *. Both **Save** and **Save As** are available on the **File** ribbon. The **Save** function is also available on the **Quick Access Toolbar** and looks like a small blue storage disk.

> **Note:** Saving often while working on a file is advisable. If your computer loses power or has technical trouble, you can lose all of your work. If you save frequently, you'll only lose the work you have done since the last save.

The Clipboard

The *Clipboard* enables you to move text or graphics within your document and between applications. Similar to the **Move to** and **Copy to** functions you used when managing files, **Cut** removes the item from the original location and places it on the Clipboard, and **Copy** makes a copy of the item, leaving the original where it is. You can use **Paste** to place both cut and copied items into a new location. A blinking cursor will indicate the insertion point for the pasted item. Allowing you to paste an item several times, the contents of the Clipboard remain there until you replace them with another selection, lock or sign out of your account, or turn off your PC.

Undo and Redo

The beauty of a word-processing program is that you can quickly correct mistakes. As you saw earlier, the **Backspace** key on your keyboard will undo a mistake in typing. But **Backspace** won't work when you make other mistakes, like accidentally cutting or pasting the wrong area, or typing over text. **Undo** and **Redo,** located on the **Quick Access Toolbar,** can help. **Undo** looks like a small arrow pointing to the left and will undo your last action. **Redo** will repeat your last action, or redo something that you just undid. Some word-processing applications allow you to undo and redo several actions, and often there is a drop down menu for the **Undo** icon, which enables you to undo several actions at once.

Print

When you are ready to commit your document to paper, you can use the **Print** function. **Print** offers several options for printing: you can print the entire document, a range of pages, the current page, or a selected part of the document. You can send the print request to a printer and have your document printed on paper, or send it to a print file for use later or to share with others. There are three print functions:

- **Print** gives you the opportunity to make some choices when printing, such as selecting the printer, the number of copies to be printed, and which pages to print.
- **Quick Print** will use the default printer and print the entire document, eliminating the need to go through the steps of making those choices.
- **Print Preview** lets you view your file on the screen to see if it looks like you want it to before you print it. This eliminates running back and forth to the printer and wasting paper as you try to get the document to look just right.

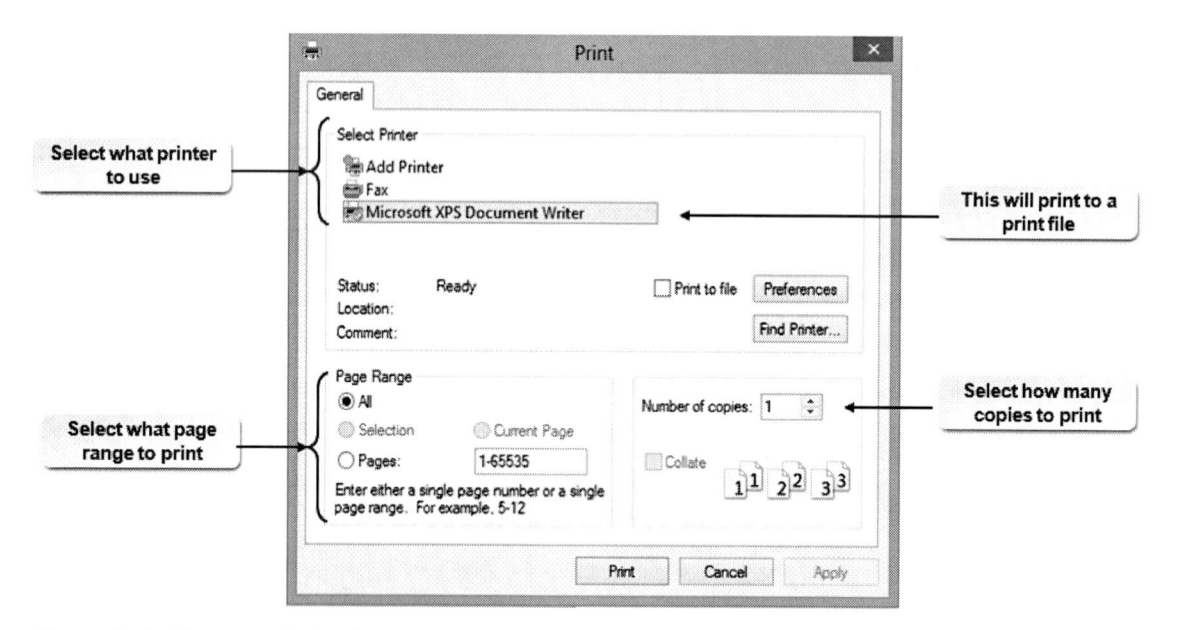

Figure 3-8: The Print dialog box.

Access the Checklist tile on your LogicalCHOICE course screen for reference information and job aids on How to Create and Modify Files Using a Desktop Application

ACTIVITY 3-4
Creating and Modifying Files with WordPad

Data Files
C:\091102Data\Working with Desktop Applications\Tents.rtf

Before You Begin
File Explorer is closed and WordPad is maximized on your screen.

Scenario
Your assistant has typed up a letter for you and you need to make changes to it. However, you'd like to practice a bit before you open the letter. Since WordPad is open and has a blank page ready, let's use this opportunity to create a new document. First, you'll enter text, then select a word and write over it. You'll use Undo and Redo to make quick corrections, then you'll save the file, assigning it a name and selecting the destination folder. At that point you'll be ready to open and modify your assistant's file, using the Clipboard to copy and paste text. These are transferable skills that will enable you to create and modify files in many applications at work and home.

---

1. Enter text in the document.
   a) Type *This is my first letter.* If you make a mistake, use **Backspace** to delete the error.

2. Replace text.
   a) Using your pointer, double-click the word "letter" to select it.

      This is my first letter.

   b) Type the word *document*. The word "letter" is replaced with "document."

      This is my first document.

3. Replace multiple words.
   a) Using your pointer, drag over the words "my first" to select them.

      This is my first document.

   b) Type *a great* to replace the words "my first" with "a great."

      This is a great document.

4. Undo an action.

a) On the **Quick Access Toolbar**, select **Undo**.
b) The words "a great" are removed and "my first" are put back.

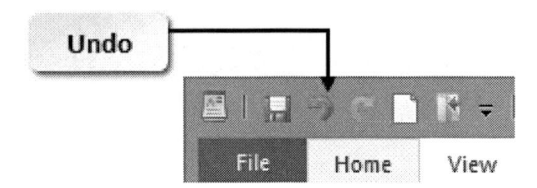

5. Redo an action.
   a) On the **Quick Access Toolbar**, select **Redo**.
   b) The words revert to "a great."

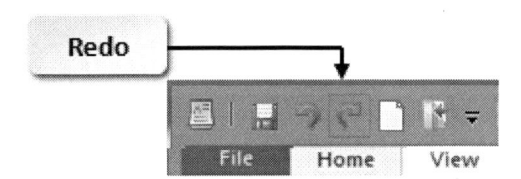

6. Save a file and select the destination folder.
   a) From the **Quick Access toolbar**, select **Save**.

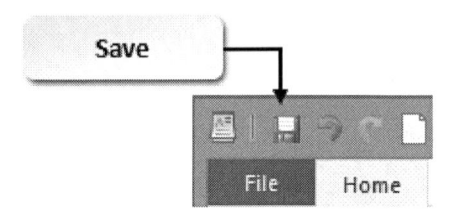

   > Note: Because this the first time you are saving this document, you need to assign a name to the file, so you are directed to the **Save As** dialog box.

   b) In the **Save As** dialog box, in the **File name** text box, verify that the word **Document** is showing and is highlighted.

   c) In the bottom right of the window, observe the **Save** and **Cancel** buttons.

   > Note: The **Cancel** button will close the dialog box and return you to your document without saving.

   d) In the **File name** text box, type *myfirst* to rename the document.

   e) In the **Contents** pane, double-click the **Letters** folder to open it.
   f) On the **Address** bar, verify that the **Letters** folder is now the destination folder.

g) Select the **Save** button. The file is saved, the **Save As** dialog box closes, and you are returned to your document.
h) On the title bar, confirm the file name **myfirst** has replaced **Document.**

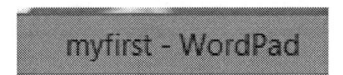

7. Open an existing file.
   a) On the **Quick Access Toolbar,** select the **Open** icon.

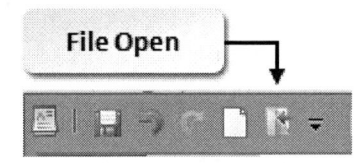

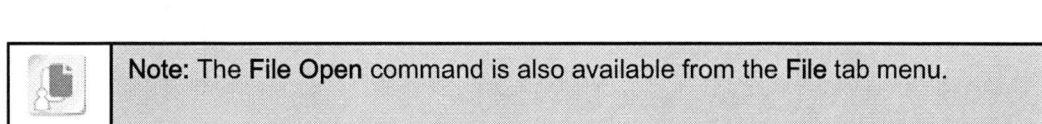

   Note: The **File Open** command is also available from the **File** tab menu.

   b) In the **Open** dialog box, on the **Address** bar, confirm that the **Letters** folder is the current folder listed.
   c) In the **Contents** pane, double-click the **Tents** file to open it.

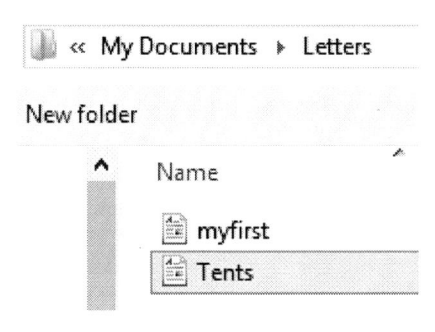

8. Use **Undo** to make a correction.
   a) Select "severe weather" and replace it with *snow* and if necessary, add a space after the word "snow."

   I'm sure you've got everything under of severe weather in Boston, so I've c
   nt posts. they would be best used.

   b) Select the **Undo** icon.
   c) Confirm that "severe weather" has returned and is still highlighted.
   d) Type *rain* to replace "severe weather." If necessary, add a space after the word "rain."

I'm sure you've got e
of rain in Boston, so
extras can go where

9. Use the Clipboard to copy and paste text.
   a) Double-click the word "Danbury" to highlight it.

   ;5k race in Danbury, CT t
   ɪ the paper that there is

   b) On the **Home** ribbon, select **Copy** to copy the word "Danbury" to the Clipboard.

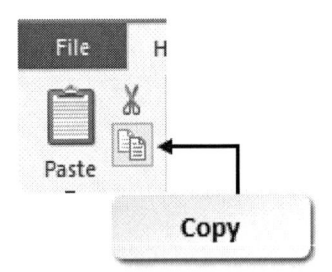

   c) Highlight the word "Boston."

   I'm sure you've got everythinɡ
   of rain in Boston, so I've ordeɪ
   extras can go wherever you fɛ

   d) Select **Paste** to replace "Boston" with the contents of the Clipboard.

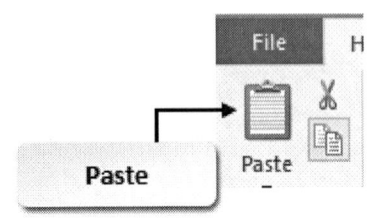

10. Save the file.
    a) On the **Quick Access Toolbar**, select the **Save** icon to replace the original file with your modified version.

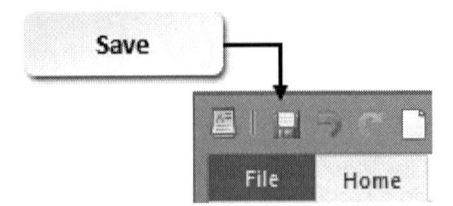

11. If you are going to do the next activity, keep your document open. If not, close the application and return to the **Start** screen.

ACTIVITY 3-5
(Optional) Printing a Document

Before You Begin
The document from the previous activity is still open.

Scenario
You're finished making changes to your document, but you'd like to make sure everything looks right before you print it out. Using Print Preview, you'll see how your document will look on the page before you print it. Then you'll open the Page Setup dialog box and change a print setting before finally printing your document.

1. Preview the document.
    a) Select the **File** tab.
    b) On the pop-up **Print** menu, select **Print preview**.

    c) Preview the document.
    d) Select anywhere on the page to zoom in on the page.
    e) Identify the groups and commands on the **Print preview** ribbon.
    f) On the **Print Preview** ribbon, select **Page setup**.

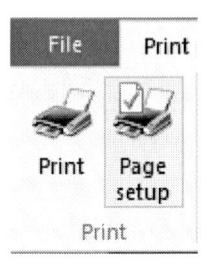

    g) If necessary, in the **Page Setup** dialog box, uncheck the **Print Page Numbers** check box.

    h) Select **OK**.
    i) On the **Print preview** ribbon, select **Close print preview** to go back to your document.

2. Print the document.
   a) From the **File** tab menu, select **Print** to open the **Print** dialog box.
   b) Identify the commands available in the **Print** dialog box.
   c) In the **Select Printer** section, select the printer you wish to use. If your PC is not connected to a printer, use Microsoft XPS Document Writer to send the document to a print file.
   d) In the **Page Range** section, verify that **All** is selected to print the entire document.
   e) Select **Print** to begin printing. You may have to assign a file name if you are printing to a print file.

3. Close WordPad.

4. Return to the **Start** screen.

Summary

In this lesson, you identified the elements of the Desktop and a typical Desktop application window. You used an application to create and edit a couple of files and learned how to save, print, and manage files and folders to help keep them organized. With this knowledge, you'll be able to create and modify documents and files at your office and at home.

What are some advantages to using applications on the Desktop?

What are the advantages to being able to create folders within folders? Are there disadvantages to having folders within folders?

> **Note:** Check your LogicalCHOICE Course screen for opportunities to interact with your classmates, peers, and the larger LogicalCHOICE online community about the topics covered in this course or other topics you are interested in. From the Course screen you can also access available resources for a more continuous learning experience.

http://www.lo-choice.com

4 Using Internet Explorer 10

Lesson Time: 1 hour

Lesson Objectives

In this lesson, you will:

- Open Internet Explorer 10 and identify what a browser is.
- Set preferences and navigate the environment.

Lesson Introduction

In Lesson 2, you used the Weather app to look at weather for different cities. Although the Weather app uses the Internet to gather information for many cities, the app is limited to showing only weather. To really be able to use the power of the Internet, you need to use an app like Internet Explorer 10. Luckily, it's bundled with Microsoft® Windows® 8 and ready for you to use.

TOPIC A

Navigate Internet Explorer 10

In today's workplace, it's imperative to be able to use the Internet to gather information, send emails, and network with colleagues. Much of what you've learned about using Modern apps and Desktop applications will help you when learning to use Internet Explorer 10.

Web Browsers and Search Engines

The words "Internet" and "World Wide Web" or "the web" are often used interchangeably, but they are not the same. The Internet is a system of interconnected networks of computers, which can be used for many things. The web is one particular use—a collection of documents and other resources that are accessed using the Internet. A *web browser* is a computer program that locates and displays information found on the web. Microsoft® Internet Explorer, Mozilla® Firefox®, Google Chrome™, and Apple® Safari® are examples of web browsers. Microsoft Bing® and Google are both examples of search engines.

Internet Explorer 10

Internet Explorer 10 (IE10) is a graphical web browser that comes bundled with Windows 8. With it, you can search the web for news, documents, images, and more. When you do a search with IE10, it sends your search request to Bing, Microsoft's search engine, which searches for websites, documents, and other resources that either contain that text, or are related to it in some way. Bing then sends the results back to Internet Explorer where they are sorted and presented on your screen, with the more relevant or popular results listed first. You can also run Internet Explorer in a Desktop window—access it by selecting the **Internet Explorer** application icon on the taskbar. IE10's default page is MSN, which is Microsoft's Internet portal. An *Internet portal* is a website that gathers information from many sources and presents it with a consistent look and feel on one website.

URL

Everything on the Internet has a unique *Uniform Resource Locator (URL)*, which is also known as an address. If you know the address of the website you are looking for, you can enter it in the **Address** bar, and IE10 will retrieve that specific page and display it on your screen.

Figure 4-1: The Internet Explorer home page.

Bing

Although you can display Bing by selecting its tile on the **Start** screen, you can also access it from Internet Explorer. The Bing home page displays a picture that changes every day. Three icons on the lower-right corner of the picture allow you to look at previous pictures, or search for information on the picture shown. As you move your pointer around the page, small squares called hotspots appear. When you hold your pointer over a hotspot, a tidbit of information related to the picture appears, along with a hyperlink (or link), which, when selected, will take you to another website or open up additional information on the current page. Whenever your pointer turns into a pointing hand, it indicates a link.

Popular Now Pane

Above the bottom command bar on the Bing home page is the **Popular now** pane, which shows news stories, images, and videos that are either currently in the news or have recently been searched for by many people. There is also a section that shows the history of your searches. The **Search History** section will be blank until you have done some searching around the web. Once items appear in your search history, you can select them to return to those pages. On the right side of the **Popular now** pane, small pictures called thumbnails provide links to images and videos that are currently popular or in the news.

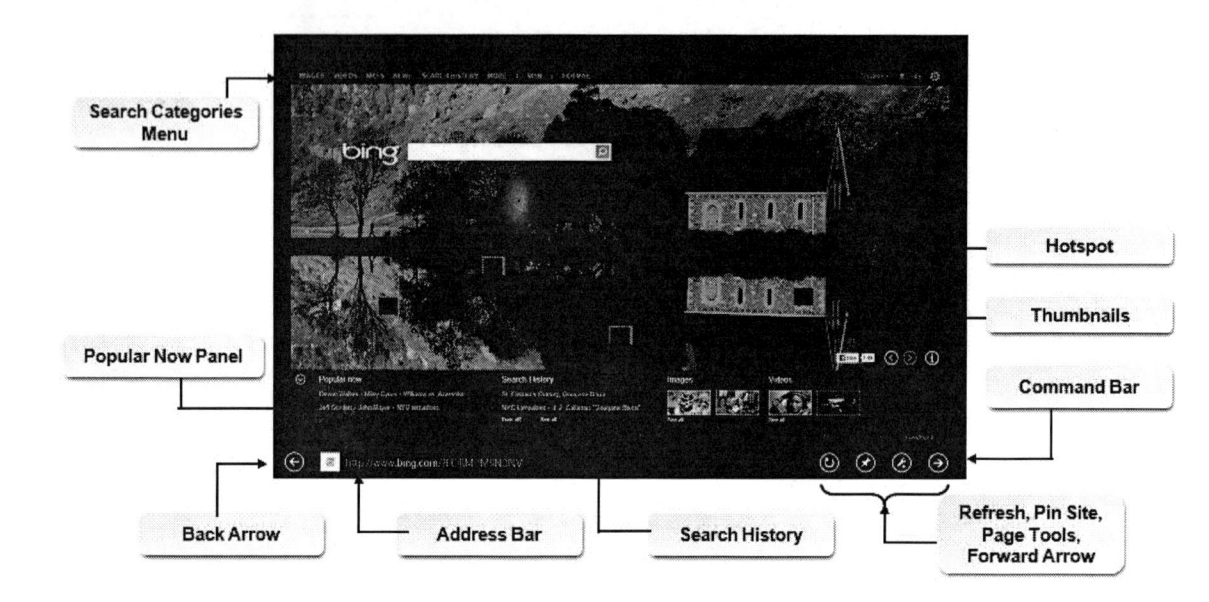

Search Categories Menu

Along the top of the Internet Explorer default page and the Bing home page are links to **Hotmail,** Microsoft's email app, and **MSN,** along with search categories such as **images, videos,** and **maps.** Each search category comes with a drop-down menu offering more specific search options for that category. A larger list of categories is accessible under **More.**

> Access the Checklist tile on your **LogicalCHOICE** course screen for reference information and job aids on **How to Navigate Internet Explorer 10 and Bing**

ACTIVITY 4-1
Navigating Internet Explorer 10

Before You Begin
You are viewing the Start screen.

Scenario
Because it is part of your job to keep abreast of trends in the news, being able to access the Internet is going to be invaluable. Before you can make full use of Internet Explorer, you need to know how to navigate around in it. Once you have mastered these skills, you'll not only be able to use them at work, but in your leisure time as well.

---

1. Open Internet Explorer.
    a) Select the Internet Explorer Tile.

    b) Verify that you are taken to the MSN home page.

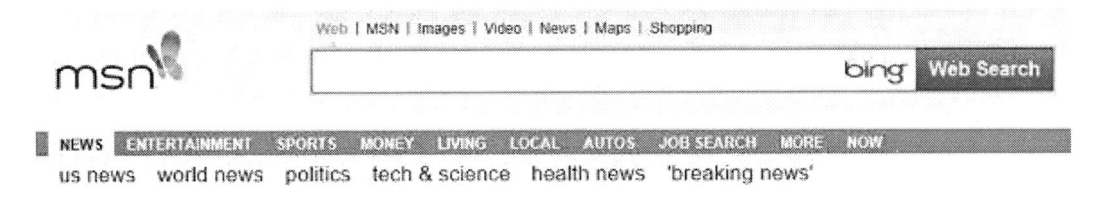

2. Navigate using **Search topics**.
    a) At the top of the page, under the MSN logo, select **news**.
    b) From the MSN News page, verify that the topics on the page offer options related to news.
    c) From the options listed under the **MSN news** logo, select **World** to navigate to a new page offering stories from around the world.

3. Navigate the page.
    a) Move your pointer over the page to identify the links available. Your pointer will look like a pointing hand when it is over a link.

b) Move your pointer over the category selections on the top of the page to reveal links related to each category.

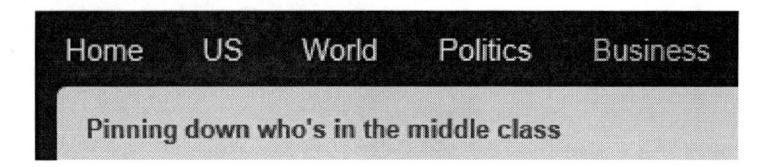

c) If necessary, use the scrollbar on the right side of the screen to view more of the page.

4. Navigate between pages.
    a) Move your pointer to the center of the left side of the screen to reveal the **Back** arrow.
    b) Select the arrow to return to the previous page.

5. Navigate to the Bing home page.
    a) In the **Search** text box, enter *Bing.com*.
    b) From the results page, select the first result, **www.bing.com**.

    Note: Because the picture changes every day, the pictures and links in the examples provided may not match the picture on your screen.

    c) Observe that the screen has icons, small images, and words in various sections.
    d) Move your pointer over the screen to activate the hotspots.
    e) Place your pointer over a hotspot to reveal a pane with information and an underlined link.
    f) Move your pointer over the link within the **Information** pane.

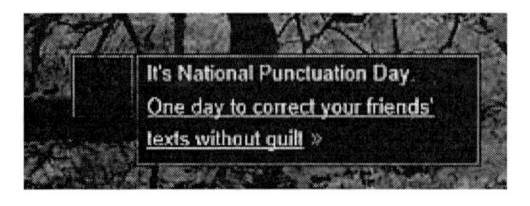

    g) Verify that the search parameters of the link appear at the bottom of your screen.

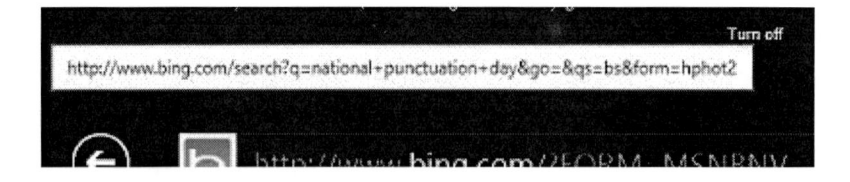

    h) In the **Information** pane, select the link to begin the search.
    i) Verify that the results on the new page are related to the link you selected.
    j) Select the **Back** arrow to go back to the previous page.
    k) Identify the **Popular now** pane. The links in this pane work the same as those of the hotspots and will begin a search for pages related to the subject indicated.

6. Navigate using a categories menu.
    a) Identify the menu bar along the top of the page.

    b) Place your pointer over **News** to open the drop-down menu.

    c) Select **See local news.**
    d) Verify that the search returns news items using your location as part of the search parameters.

7. Use the **Back** arrow to return to the Bing home page.

TOPIC B

Browse the Web

You've seen how to move around and use the search links provided on the IE home page, but the real power of the Internet is being able to specify your own search criteria. In your work, having the resources of the Internet at your fingertips will be invaluable.

The Search Bar

Although you can perform a search within Internet Explorer and Bing using the **Search Charm**, you can also use the **Search** bar. The **Search** bar is the text box located at the top or near the top of the page. To perform a search, you enter a word or phrase into the **Search** bar text box and the search engine scans for websites, documents, and other resources that have that word or phrase, or are related to it. The search engine then returns the results for your browser to display. The more specific your query, the better your results will be.

Search Suggestions

To use search suggestions, just begin typing in the **Search** bar. As you type, Internet Explorer tries to predict what you are looking for and offers a list of suggestions based on what you've typed, previous searches you have done, and similar searches that it has found on the Internet. If the list includes the term you intended to type into the **Search** bar text box, you can save time by selecting the suggestion to begin your search. Search suggestions can be turned on and off from the **Preferences** menu, discussed later in this topic.

Figure 4-2: Search suggestions in Internet Explorer.

> Access the Checklist tile on your LogicalCHOICE course screen for reference information and job aids on How to Use the Search Bar

The Command Bar

As with the other apps provided by Windows 8, IE10 has hidden command bars. When you first open the app, the command bar along the bottom of the screen is visible, but will disappear when you select anywhere on the page. When you need to use it again, simply right-click the background of the screen to bring it back.

The following table describes the elements of the IE10 command bar.

Element	Action
Address bar	Shows the address of the page you're on, and allows you to enter a specific website address to navigate to that site.
Back arrow	Located on the left side of the command bar, the **Back** arrow takes you back to the previous page.
Forward arrow	Located on the right side of the command bar, the **Forward** arrow takes you forward a page. **Forward** and **Back** take you only to pages you have viewed in the current session.
Refresh icon	Tells your computer to reload the page you're on. This can be helpful when the browser is running slow, or on pages where information is fluid and may be updated in real time.
Page Tools icon	Enables you to search for text on the current page, or to view IE10 in a Desktop window.
Pin Site icon	Lets you pin the current page to **Start,** or add it to your **Favorites** list. Both options give you a quick way to access sites that you visit frequently.

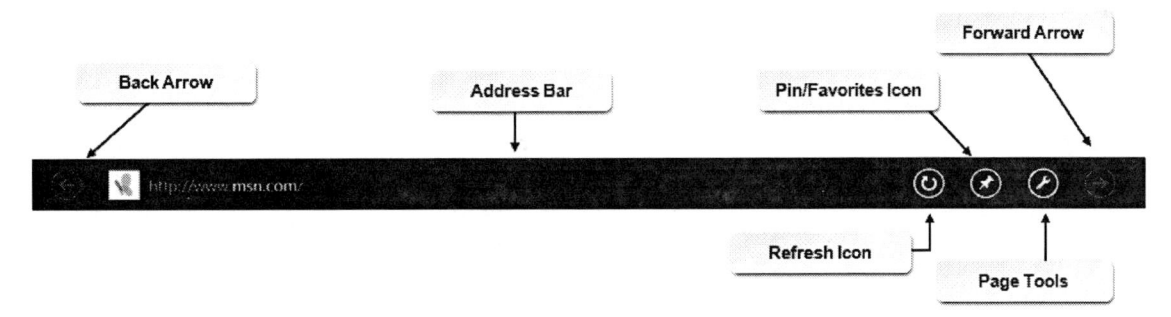

Figure 4-3: The Internet Explorer command bar.

The Quick Site Access Panel

Selecting the **Address** bar will display the **Quick Site Access Panel**, which displays links to sites that you visit frequently, along with links to sites that you have designated as favorites. Selecting one of these links will take you directly to the site listed on the link. This menu is available at all times when in Internet Explorer.

Figure 4-4: The Quick Site Access Panel.

> Access the Checklist tile on your LogicalCHOICE course screen for reference information and job aids on How to Use Icons on the Command Bar, and the Quick Site Access Panel

The Tabs Menu

Internet Explorer lets you use more than one page at a time by using tabs. This allows you to do more than one search at a time and keeps the history of each search separate. You can open and manage tabs using the **Tabs** menu, a hidden command bar at the top of the page. This command bar shows what tabs are open and which tab you are currently using, and provides a means of switching between tabs. There is always one tab open during your browsing session, and you can have up to 10 tabs open at once. Each tab has a **Close Tab** icon for closing it individually.

Also on the menu are the **New Tab** and **Tab Tools** icons. The **New Tab** icon will open a new tab, while the **Tab Tools** icon provides a menu where you can either close all of the tabs (except for the current page) or open an **InPrivate** tab. Using an **InPrivate** tab temporarily prevents Internet Explorer from storing data about the browsing session for that tab.

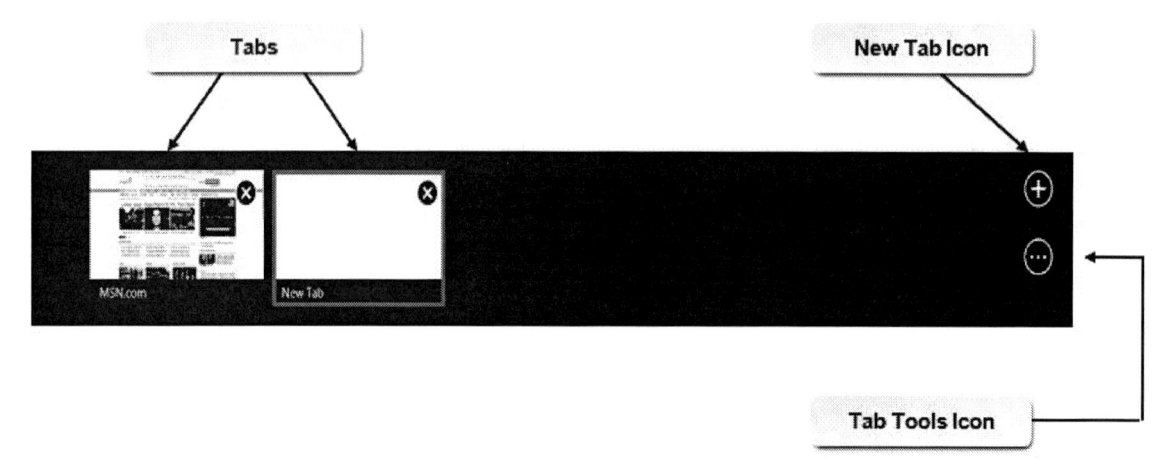

Figure 4-5: The Tabs menu.

> Access the Checklist tile on your LogicalCHOICE course screen for reference information and job aids on How to Use Tabs

Preferences

The small gear at the top right of your screen provides a link to your preferences. Preferences allow you to change settings for browsing, such as filtering out unsafe text, images, and videos; allowing the browser to make suggestions based on your location or the text you type into the **Search** box; and what language to use when displaying results. You can also turn search history on or off, and view or clear your search history.

> **Note:** To further explore Search History on the **Preferences** menu, you can access the LearnTO **Manage Your Online Search History** presentation from the **LearnTO** tile on the LogicalCHOICE Course screen.

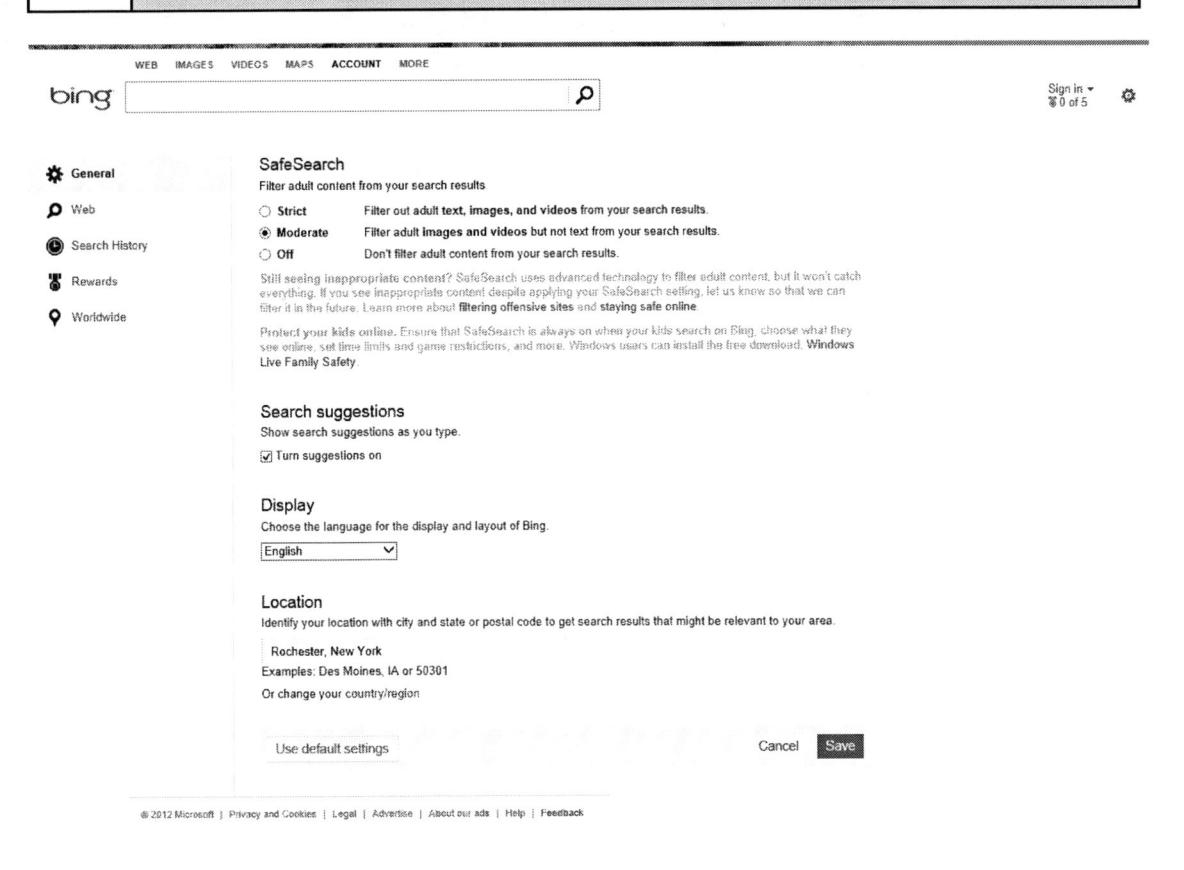

Figure 4-6: The Preferences page.

> Access the Checklist tile on your LogicalCHOICE course screen for reference information and job aids on **How to Set Preferences**

The Share Charm

Using the **Share Charm**, you can quickly share the address or content of a website; pictures from your photo gallery; or content from an app with your Mail contacts, another app, or—once you set up connections—your accounts on social networking sites such as LinkedIn, Facebook, or Twitter. The **Share Charm** works with Windows 8 apps that support the function, but not Desktop applications or the **Start** screen. To see if the **Share** feature works with the app you are using, from the **Charms** menu, select the **Share Charm**.

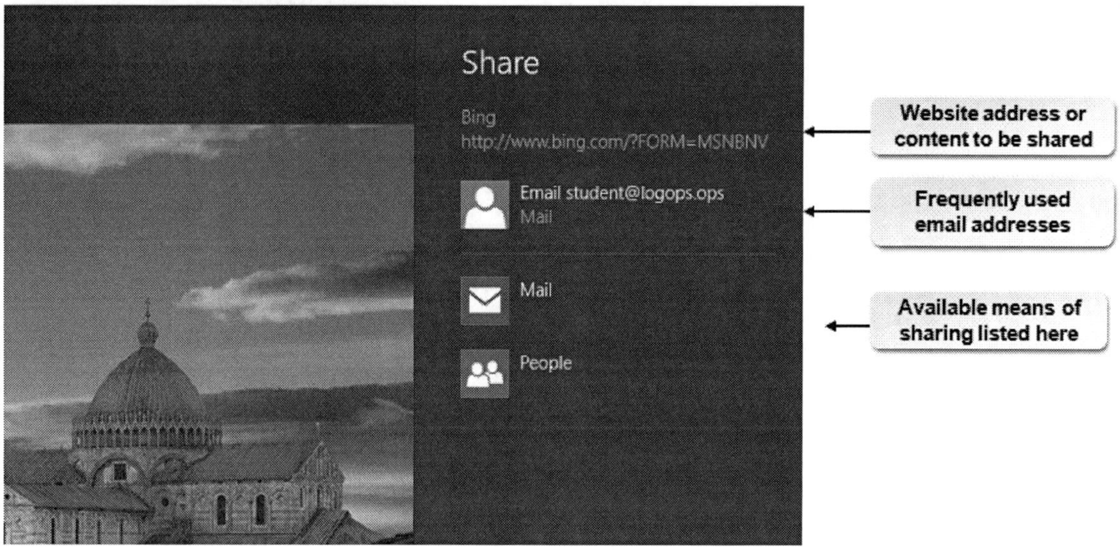

Figure 4-7: Sharing in Internet Explorer.

> Access the Checklist tile on your LogicalCHOICE course screen for reference information and job aids on How to Share

ACTIVITY 4-2
Using Internet Explorer and Share

Before You Begin
You are at the Bing home page on Internet Explorer.

Scenario
On your upcoming business trip to Boston, you'd like to visit a museum and have lunch at a café with a colleague. In preparation, you'll search online for museums in the Boston area and save a museum site as a favorite. This will enable you to return to the site without having to search again. Keeping the search results handy, you'll open a second tab to conduct a search of Boston's cafés. Finally, you'll share the list of cafés you find with your colleague so she can help in choosing where to go.

---

1. Conduct a search.
   a) In the **Search** bar, type *Boston museums*
   b) Verify that the suggestions listed below change to fit your search terms as you type.
   c) From the suggestion list, select **Boston museums**.

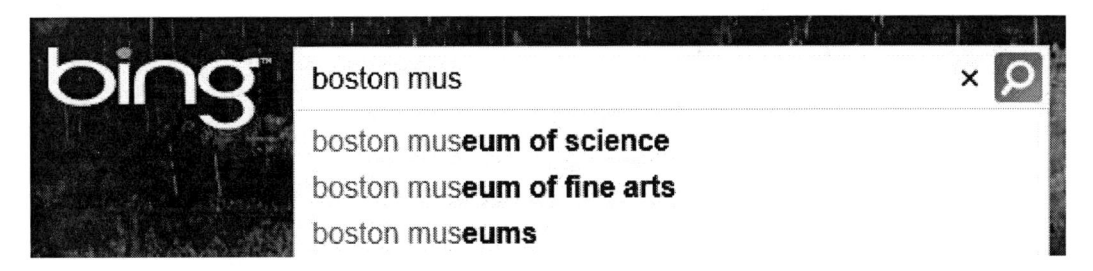

   d) Verify that there are several links listed that will take you to different websites on Boston museums.
   e) In the **Search** bar, confirm that your search term is still listed.

2. Redefine the search.
   a) Add the word *maps* to your search term and press **Enter** to begin another search.

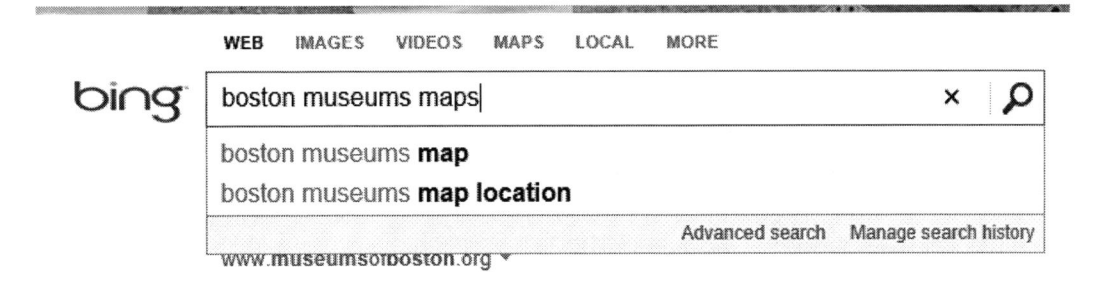

   b) Observe that the new search results provide links to sites with maps of Boston's museums.
   c) Select **Museums of Boston** to go to that website.

WEB   IMAGES   VIDEOS   MAPS   LOCAL   MORE

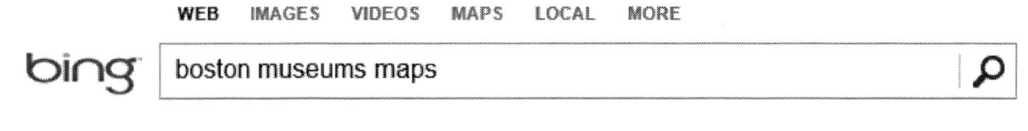

bing boston museums maps

53,300,000 RESULTS

Museums of Boston
www.**museumsofboston**.org
Museums of **Boston** is a collaborative organization of over 40 Greater ... **Museums** of **Boston** Members in a larger **map**

3. Pin the site as a favorite.
    a) Right-click to open the command bar.
    b) On the command bar, select the **Pin Site** icon.
    c) Select **Add to favorites.** This site is now listed as one of your favorites.

4. View the **Quick Site Access Panel**.
    a) Select the **Address** bar to open the **Quick Site Access Panel**. The museum website is listed under the **Favorites** title. If necessary, use the scroll bar on the bottom to view favorites.

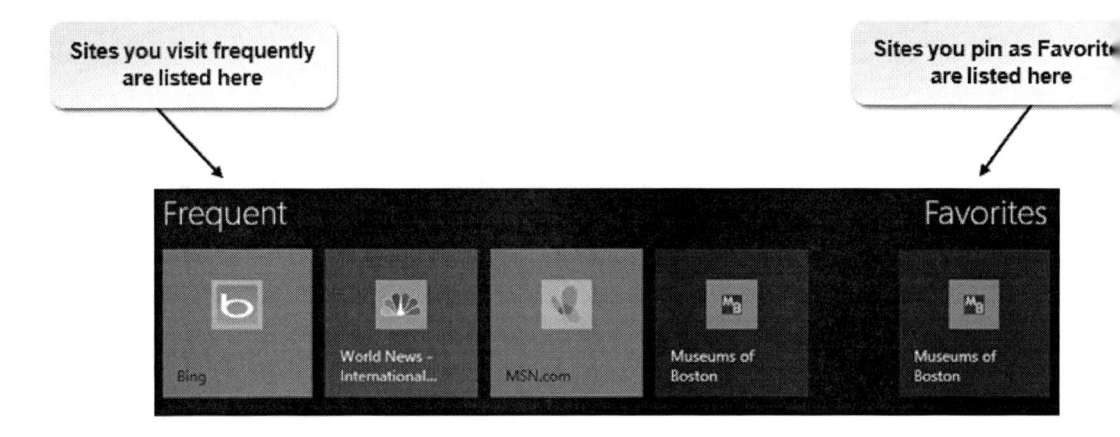

    b) Select the background of the website page to close the **Favorites** menu.

5. Open a second tab and perform a search.
    a) Right-click the background area of the search page to open the **Tabs** menu.
    b) Select the **New Tab** icon to open a new tab.

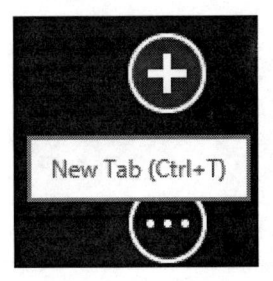

c) Verify that the page is blank and the **Quick Site Access Panel** is displayed.
d) In the **Search** bar text box at the bottom of the page, type *cafés in Boston*
e) Above the **Search** text box, verify that suggestions are listed.

f) Select the **Go** icon or press **Enter** to begin your search.
g) Confirm that the results of your search are presented on the page.

6. Refine your search.
    a) Under the **Search** bar, select **Cuisine**.

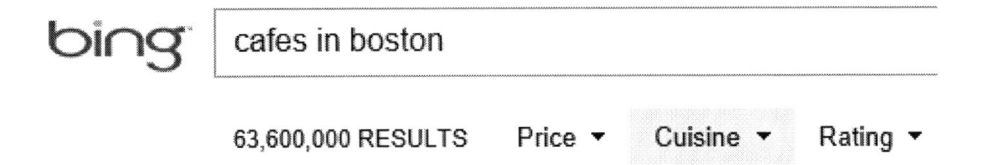

    b) From the drop-down list, select **Seafood** to view only cafés that serve seafood.
    c) Confirm that the results returned are further refined.

7. Share a link to a web page.
    a) From the **Charms** menu, select **Share**.
    b) Verify that the choices offered are **Mail** and **People**.
    c) Select **Mail**.

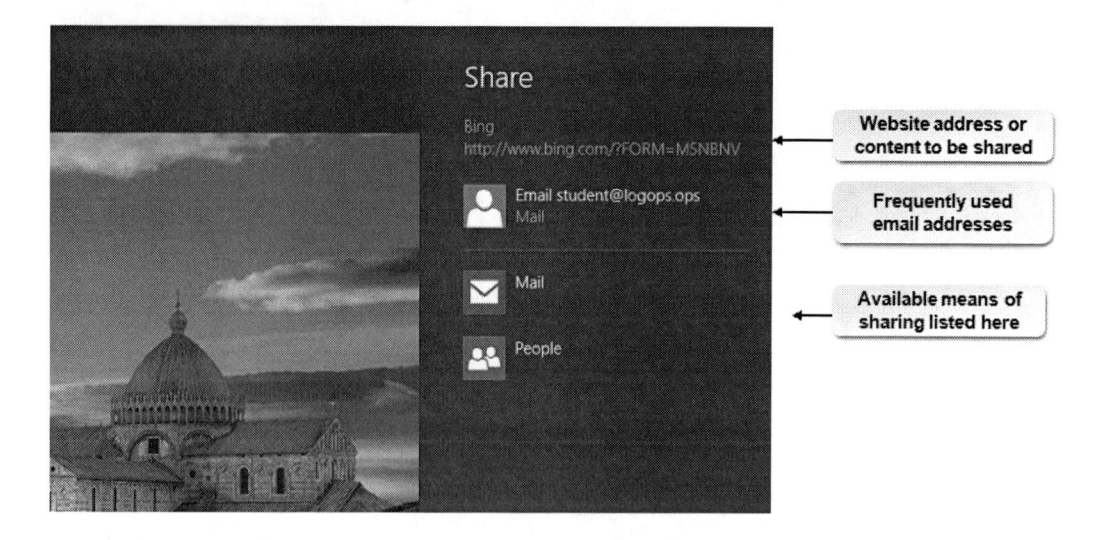

Callouts on the Share screenshot:
- Website address or content to be shared
- Frequently used email addresses
- Available means of sharing listed here

d) Identify the elements of the page.
e) The subject is cafes in boston.
f) There is room to add a message.
g) Below the message area is the address for the search results you are sharing.

Add a message

Sent from Windows Mail

cafes in boston - Bing
http://www.bing.com/entities/search?q=cafes+in+boston&filters=segment%3a%22l...
http://www.bing.com/entities/search?q=cafes+in+boston&filters=segment%3a%22local%22+ex2%3a%22e5%22&src=IE-TopResult&qpvt=cafes+in+boston

h) Your email address is at the top of the page.
i) In the **To** text box, type the email address provided by your instructor.
j) Select the **Send** button to send the email.

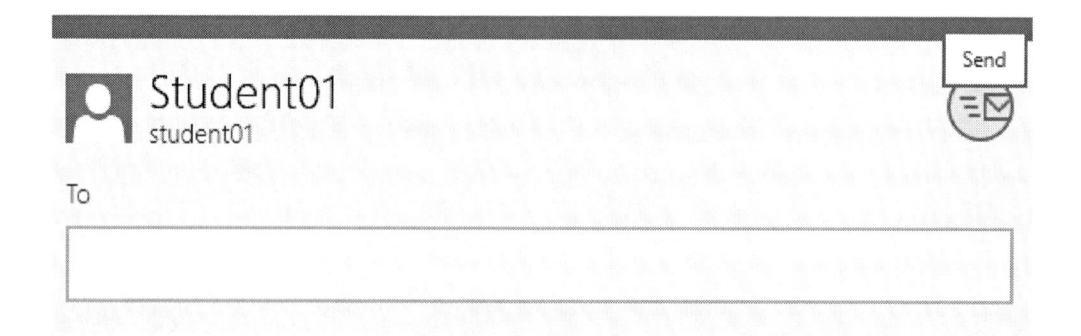

Student01
student01

To

8. Close **Share**.
   a) Select the background area of the search page to close **Share** and return to the search.

9. Close the café search tab.
   a) Right-click the page background to open the **Tabs** menu.
   b) Verify that there are two tabs open: one shows the museum page from the museum search, and the other shows the results of the café search.
   c) Select the **Close Tab** button to close the café tab.

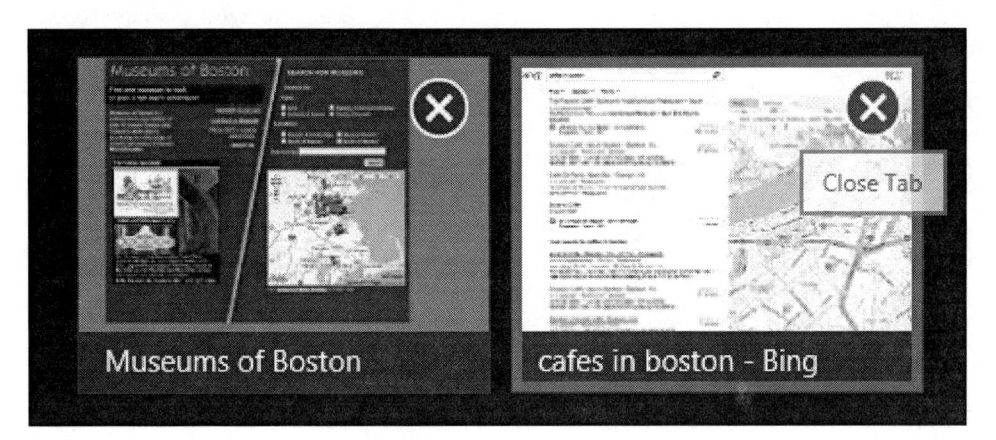

   d) Verify that you have returned to the museum page.
   e) Select the background of the museum page to close the **Tabs** menu.

10. Return to the **Start** screen.

Summary

In this lesson, you opened Internet Explorer 10 and learned how to search the web and share your results. You also learned how to use multiple tabs, navigate between pages, and set preferences and favorites. With these skills, you'll be able to customize your searches to utilize the many resources on the Internet in your workplace and in your personal life.

How might the Share Charm help you in your job?

How do you think being able to search the Internet might be helpful in your job?

> **Note:** Check your LogicalCHOICE Course screen for opportunities to interact with your classmates, peers, and the larger LogicalCHOICE online community about the topics covered in this course or other topics you are interested in. From the Course screen you can also access available resources for a more continuous learning experience.

http://www.lo-choice.com

5 | Customizing the Windows 8 Environment

Lesson Time: 1 hour

Lesson Objectives

In this lesson, you will:

- Customize the look of the Start screen.
- Customize the look of the Desktop and Desktop applications.

Lesson Introduction

Just like your office at work, it's nice to be able to customize your PC so that it fits the way you work and reflects your personality. With Microsoft® Windows® 8, you can change the colors on your screen, make your pointer easier to work with, make the layout of Start more efficient, and control the devices connected to your PC.

TOPIC A

Customize the Start Screen

As you work with Windows 8 and add more apps, you'll probably want to organize the tiles to make finding apps easier. You may even want to personalize your PC by changing the look of the Lock screen, the Start screen, and your Account ID photo. In addition, you'll probably be adding peripherals to your PC or want to clear your search history.

Tile Groups

Tiles on the **Start** screen are laid out in groups, and in the initial setup of Windows 8, there are two groups of tiles. As you add apps and pin them to **Start,** this layout may get a bit disorganized. To make tiles easier to find, you can group similar or often-used tiles together in one group, and give the group a name. You can rearrange groups on the **Start** screen, and add or remove tiles from groups as needed. Selecting the **Semantic Zoom** button will zoom out the **Start** screen so you can see all tiles pinned to it. This is handy when you have more tiles than will fit on one screen. This also allows you to assign names to the groups using the **Name Groups** command bar, and move groups of tiles around.

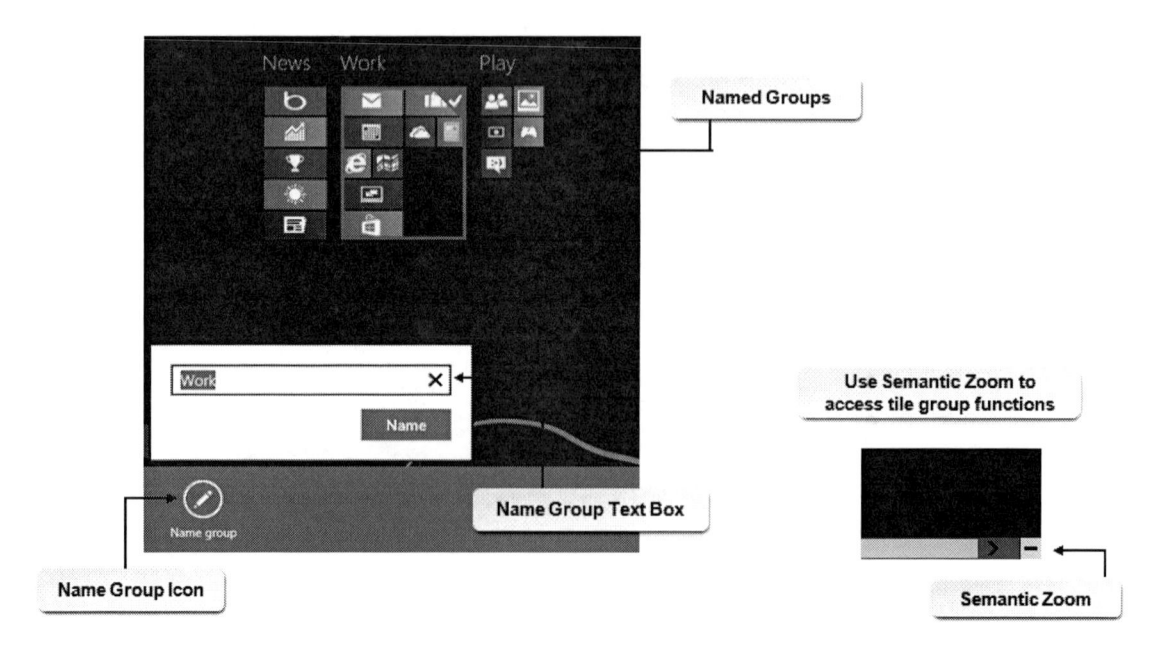

Figure 5-1: Tile groups.

> Access the Checklist tile on your LogicalCHOICE course screen for reference information and job aids on How to Create and Name Tile Groups

ACTIVITY 5-1
Creating Groups on the Start Screen

Scenario
In your work, you will probably add apps to the Start screen, and you may find that you use some apps more than others. Organizing and labeling groups of tiles will make finding and opening apps much easier in your everyday endeavors. You will organize the apps into related groups by dragging the tiles to new positions on the Start screen. You will then assign a name to one of the groups and move the group to a new position on your screen.

1. Create a new group.
   a) Drag the **News, Weather, Finance,** and **Sports** tiles to the right to form a new group.
   b) Make the **Finance** tile larger.
   c) Drag the rest of the tiles to the left into the group with **Desktop** and **Mail**.
   d) You should now have two groups of tiles.

2. Name the group.
   a) Use the **Semantic Zoom** button to zoom out the **Start** screen and view all groups.

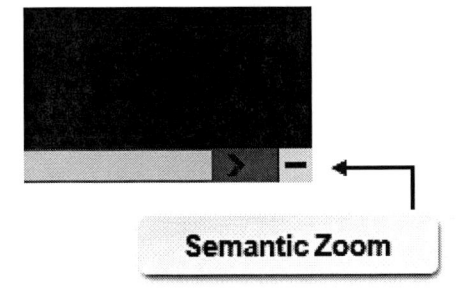

   b) Right click the smaller group.

c) Verify that the group is outlined and has a small check in the top-right corner.

d) On the command bar, select **Name group**.

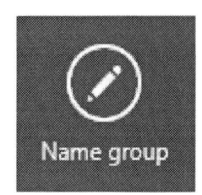

e) In the **Name Group** text box, type *News* and select **Name**.

f) Confirm the name **News** appears over the second group.
g) Select anywhere on the background to return **Start** to normal.
h) Verify that the smaller group is now named **News**.

3. Move the group.
   a) Zoom out the **Start** screen to view all groups.
   b) Drag the **News** group to the left side of the screen. The other group will move to accommodate the new location.

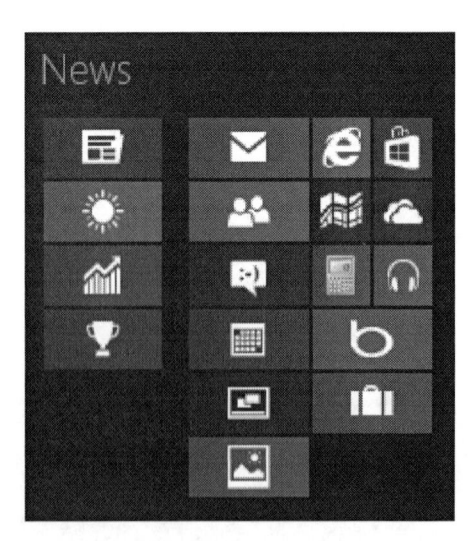

c) Select anywhere on the screen to return **Start** to full size.
d) Confirm that the groups are rearranged and the **News** group is now the group on the left.

The Settings Charm

Like the other Charms, the **Settings Charm** is context sensitive and offers different options depending on where you are when you open it. On the **Start** screen, the **Settings Charm** lets you clear any personal information from your **Start** tiles. This doesn't turn live tiles off, but resets the tiles to their default state. No matter where you are, the **Settings Charm** enables you to perform several actions:

- Access **Shut down** options.
- View Wi-Fi signal strength and connect to a network.
- Adjust speaker volume.
- Change the frequency of notifications.
- Access the onscreen keyboard.
- Adjust the brightness of your monitor.
- Access **Help**.

Change PC Settings

Accessed through the **Settings Charm, Change PC settings** is a collection of menus that gives you control over many aspects of how your PC looks and works. From the appearance of the **Start** screen to adding new users or devices, the **PC settings** menu gives you access to menus for changing time zone and language, limiting what apps to use with the **Search Charm,** deleting search history, changing passwords and privacy settings, and much more.

Like Desktop File Explorer, the **PC settings** menu has a **Navigation** pane displaying submenus on the left side of the screen, and a **Contents** pane on the right displaying the actions available for the selected submenu.

Menu	Uses
Personalize	Allows you to change the pictures used for the **Lock** and **Start** screen backgrounds, as well as your **Account ID**. Also allows you to choose which apps can post status and notifications on the **Lock** screen.
Users	Allows you to change your password and set up PIN and picture passwords, and set whether passwords must be used when resuming from sleep mode. Also enables you to add user accounts to the PC.
Notifications	Enables you to turn app notifications on or off, and indicate which apps may show notifications. Also lets you turn notification sounds on or off.
Search	Allows you to show frequently used apps at the top during searches, and use past searches in future search suggestions. Enables you to exclude apps from searches and delete search history in Windows.
Share	Allows you to show apps you use most often at the top of the list when sharing, and limit how many are listed. Lets you exclude apps from sharing.
General	Enables you to set your time zone, and have the PC automatically adjust for daylight saving time. Allows you to adjust settings for switching between apps, set language, turn on Spelling autocorrect/highlighting, and view available storage. Also allows you to refresh or reinstall Windows, or start your PC from a disc.

Menu	Uses
Privacy	Lets you control whether apps can use your location, name, and account picture, and whether Microsoft can use the URLs from websites you use to help select apps for the Windows Store.
Devices	Enables you to add and remove devices such as printers, monitors, keyboards, and external storage devices from your PC. Some devices, such as flash drives, need to be properly prepared before being physically removed from your PC.
Ease of Access	Allows you to set **Ease of Access** features such as **High Contrast monitor, Narrator, Magnifier, On-screen keyboard**, and cursor thickness. Also lets you adjust how long notifications remain on your screen.
Sync your settings	If you are signed on to your Microsoft Account, this enables you to sync settings on multiple PCs so that each one is set up the same as the others, letting you work in a consistent and familiar environment no matter what machine you are on.
HomeGroup	This enables you to connect two or more PCs on a home network in order to share printers, media, and document libraries.
Windows Update	Although Windows is set up to automatically search for and install updates, this allows you to manually check for updates.

Note: You can also remove flash drives and other external storage devices via the Notification area on the Desktop.

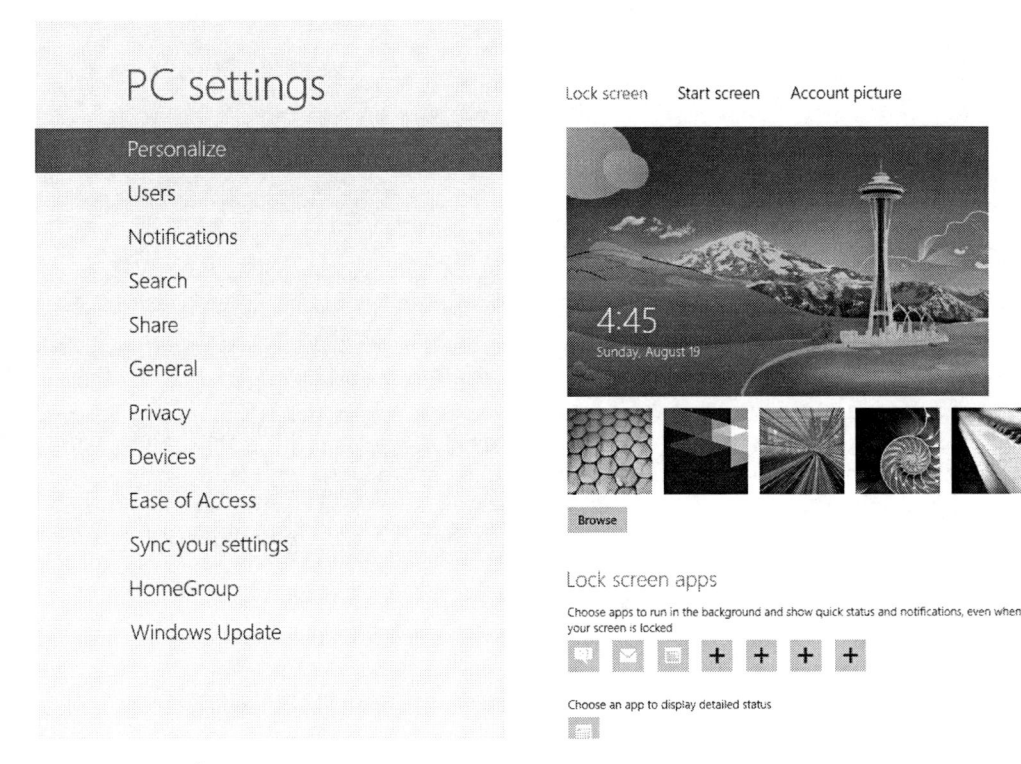

Figure 5-2: The PC settings menu.

Access the Checklist tile on your LogicalCHOICE course screen for reference information and job aids on How to Change Common Elements of the Windows 8 Environment

ACTIVITY 5-2
Changing PC Settings

Before You Begin
Have your password handy, as you will be locking your account during this activity and you will need it to sign back in to your account.

Scenario
You customized the Start screen by grouping tiles and arranging and naming the groups. Now, you'll continue to customize Windows 8 by changing the backgrounds for the Lock and Start screens, adding an app notification to the Lock screen, selecting your time zone, and clearing all of your personal info from live tiles. These changes can make using Windows 8 more enjoyable and useful.

1. Access the **Change PC settings** menu.
   a) Select the **Settings Charm**.
   b) On the bottom of the **Settings** menu, select **Change PC settings** to open the **PC settings** menu.

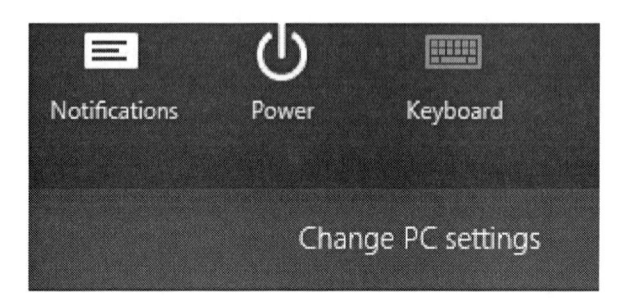

   c) In the **Navigation** pane, confirm that **Personalize** is highlighted, indicating it is the active menu.
   d) Verify that the large picture in the example area shows how the **Lock** screen currently looks.

2. Change the **Lock** screen background picture.
   a) At the top of the **Contents** pane, verify that **Lock screen** is selected. It's a different color than the other two options.

   Lock screen   Start screen   Account picture

   b) Following the example picture, view the optional pictures supplied for that screen.
   c) Select each of the smaller pictures to see how the **Lock** screen will look with that picture.
   d) Select the picture you wish to use for the **Lock** screen background.

3. Add an app notification to appear on the **Lock** screen.
   a) Under **Lock screen apps,** select the **plus** icon to display detailed status.
   b) From the pop-up menu, select the **Weather** app.

Lock screen apps

Choose apps to run in the background and show quick status and notifications, even when your screen is locked

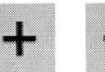

c) Verify that the **Weather** icon now appears in the fourth slot for **Lock screen apps**.

Lock screen apps

Choose apps to run in the background and show quick status and notifications, even when your screen is locked

d) Select the icon under **Choose an app to display detailed status**.

Choose an app to display detailed status

e) From the pop-up menu, select **Weather**.

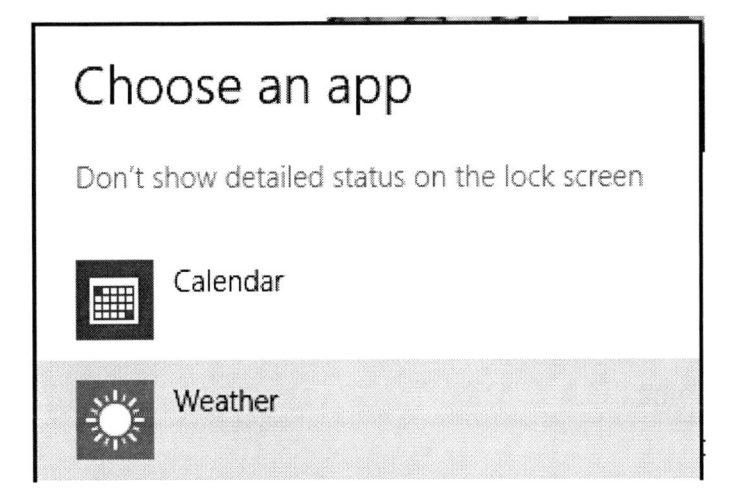

Choose an app

Don't show detailed status on the lock screen

Calendar

Weather

4. Change the **Start** screen background.
   a) At the top of the **Contents** pane, select **Start screen**.

   Lock screen   Start screen   Account picture

   b) Below the example area, verify that there is an assortment of stylized graphics and colors.
   c) Select the graphics to see how the **Start** screen would look with a different graphic.

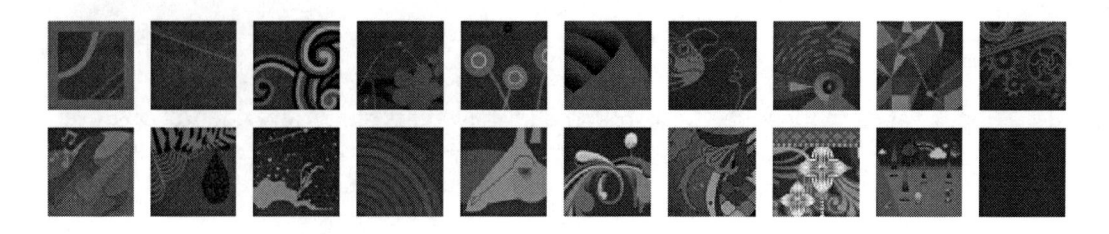

d) Below the graphics option bar, observe the color bar.
e) Select some of the color options to see the **Start** screen using different colors.

f) Select the graphic and color option you wish to use for the **Start** screen background.

> **Note:** Your changes are automatically saved.

5. Return to **Start**.
   a) Verify that the **Start** screen has a new look using the selections you chose.

6. Lock your account to view the changes to the **Lock** screen.
   a) Select your **Account ID** to open the menu.
   b) Select **Lock**.
   c) Verify that the new picture you chose is now the **Lock** screen background.
   d) Confirm that detailed weather information is displayed next to the time.

7. Change the time zone.
   a) Select anywhere on the **Lock** screen and sign in to your account.
   b) From the **Settings Charm**, select **Change PC settings**.
   c) In the **Navigation** pane, select **General**.
   d) Under **Time**, select the time zone drop-down list to display the time zones available.

   # Time

   5:19 AM, Tuesday, October 9, 2012

   (UTC-08:00) Pacific Time (US & Canada)

   e) From the options listed, select your time zone. If necessary, use the scroll bar on the right side of the menu to view your time zone.

8. Set your PC to automatically adjust for daylight saving time.
   a) If necessary, select the switch below the time zone to toggle it to **On**.

   Adjust for daylight saving time automatically
   On

9. Return to **Start** to save your changes.

10. Display the **Charms** menu to view the time. If you had to change time zones, the new time should now be displayed.

11. Clear personal information from live tiles.
    a) Open the **Settings Charm**.
    b) Under **Settings,** select **Tiles**.

    Settings
    Start
    Tiles
    Help

    c) Select **Clear** to clear personal information from the tiles.

    ← Tiles

    Show administrative tools
    No

    Clear personal info from my tiles
    Clear

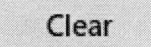

    d) Verify that the tiles are reset.
    e) Close the menu to return to **Start.**

TOPIC B

Customize the Desktop

Besides changing the Lock and Start screens, you can also change the background picture on the Desktop, as well as the color of application window borders. The Desktop is also the place to go to change how your pointer looks and responds.

Desktop Background

When you open the Desktop, the background shows the default picture that comes with Windows 8. You can change the background picture by using other pictures bundled with Windows 8, or by using your own pictures. You can select one picture to be displayed, or have several displayed as a slide show, with the interval between pictures ranging from 10 seconds to 1 day. Windows 8 also offers high-contrast backgrounds, for easier-to-see, less-cluttered viewing. Pictures can be positioned on your screen in the numerous ways:

- **Fill**—The picture will fill the entire screen. Some stretching or picture loss may occur.
- **Fit**—The picture will fit the screen horizontally, but may have black areas above and below.
- **Stretched**—The picture will be stretched to cover the screen top to bottom or side to side.
- **Centered**—The picture will be centered on your screen with black on all sides.
- **Tiled**—Many small copies of the picture will cover the screen in a tiled fashion.

Border and Taskbar Color

You can also change the color and intensity of the borders of windows and the taskbar. Windows 8 offers 16 different colors to choose from. Changing the window color will affect the title bar, borders, and taskbar. You can save picture and border color combinations as **Themes,** making switching between customizations easier.

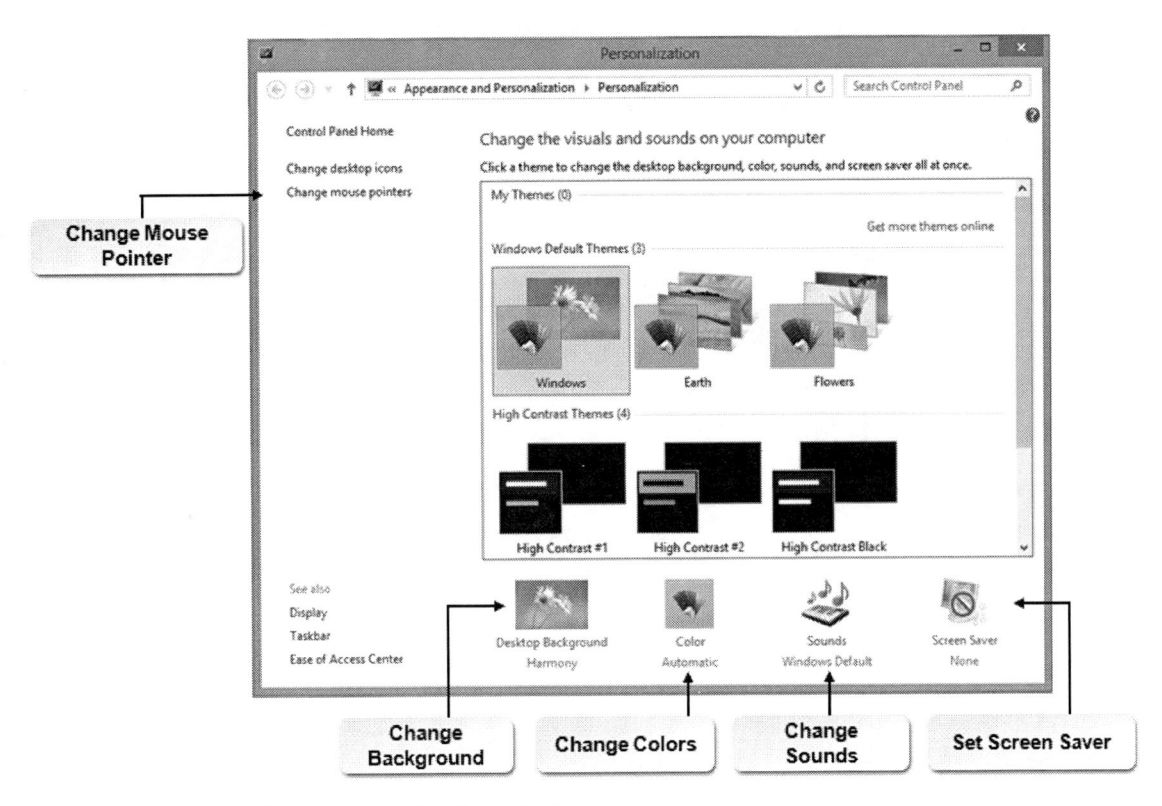

Figure 5-3: The Desktop Personalization window.

Screen Savers

With early models of PCs and monitors, if you left a static image on your monitor for too long, the image would burn into your screen. To combat this, *screen savers* were developed. Screen savers provide either a blank screen, or a constant changing of images or words on your monitor. This constant refreshing of your monitor prevents image burn. When your computer has not been used for a specified amount of time, the screen saver will start up and will continue to be displayed until you either move your mouse or press a key on your keyboard. Image burn isn't as much a problem with modern PCs, as they have sleep mode, which blanks out the monitor after a specified amount of time. However, some people still like to use screen savers.

Note: Screen savers don't really serve a purpose anymore, they're just fun.

Access the Checklist tile on your LogicalCHOICE course screen for reference information and job aids on How to Customize the Desktop

Pointers

When you first use Windows, the default pointer shape is a white arrow. As your pointer moves over aspects of the screen, it changes shape according to the field or action that you can perform. To make viewing and tracking the pointer easier, you can change the size, shape, and color of your pointer. You can also set it so that your pointer has a shadow or has pointer trails. With pointer trails, whenever you move your pointer you will see several pointers "following" it. This makes it easier for your eyes to track the pointer movement. You can also set the pointer to move faster or slower in relation to your mouse movement. Use the **Mouse Properties** dialog box to change other pointer properties, such as button configuration and click speed.

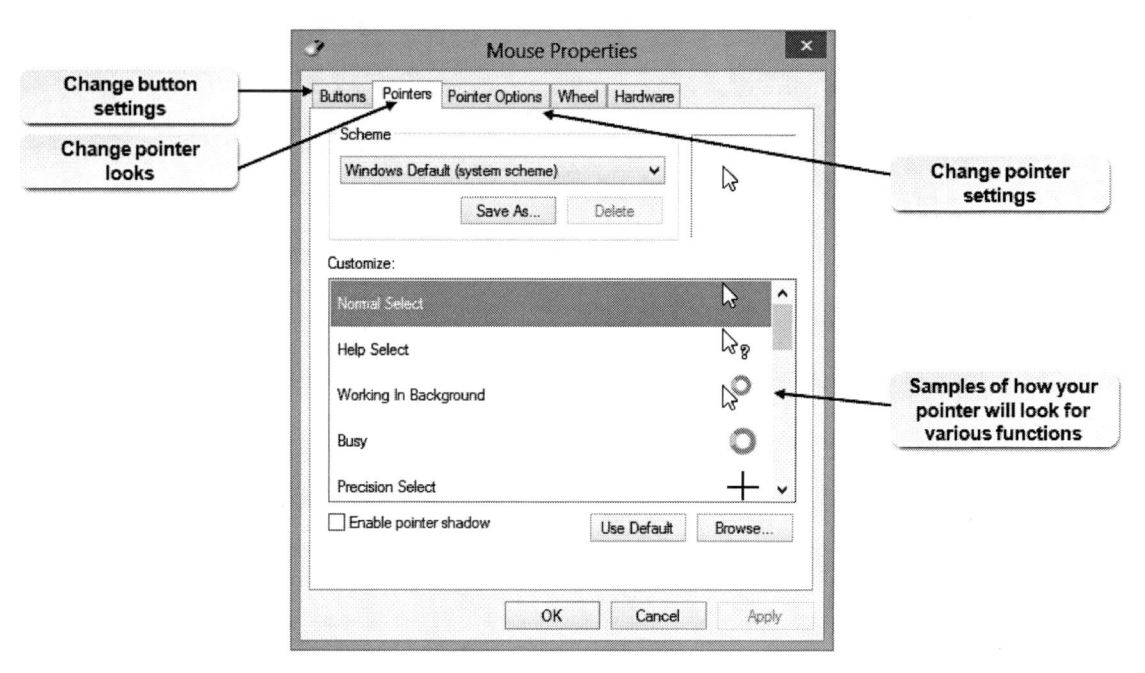

Figure 5-4: The Mouse Properties dialog box.

> Access the Checklist tile on your LogicalCHOICE course screen for reference information and job aids on How to Customize Your Pointer

ACTIVITY 5-3
Personalizing the Desktop

Before You Begin
You are on the Start screen.

Scenario
Studies have shown that when you personalize your workspace, you enjoy work more and work more efficiently. Since your PC will be used so much during your work day, it makes sense to personalize your PC and make it easier and more pleasing to use. You start by changing the background picture on the Desktop and selecting a screen saver. You may find that you'd like to change the look of your pointer, or change how fast it responds to your mouse movements. You decide to take a look at some of the changes you can make to your pointer.

1. Change the Desktop background.
    a) Select the **Desktop** tile to open the Desktop app.
    b) On the Desktop, select the **Settings Charm.**
    c) Select **Personalization.**

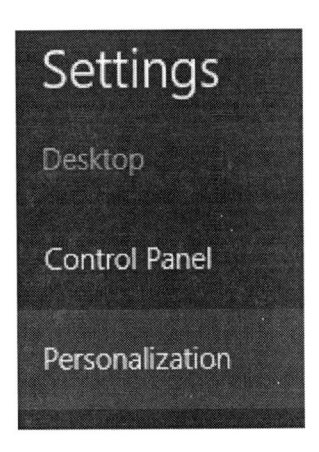

    d) Select **Desktop Background** to view the Windows 8 default pictures.

    Desktop Background
    Harmony

    e) In the sample window section, scroll up to view all pictures available.
    f) Select a picture from the available pictures.

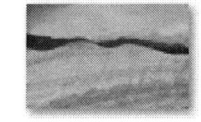

g) Verify that the Desktop changes to show how the picture will look.

> **Note:** You may want to minimize the window to view the new picture on the Desktop. Restore the window when you are done viewing the Desktop. Also, notice that the sample pictures have their own themes, which changes the color of the taskbar and your window borders when you use these pictures.

h) When you have chosen a picture to use, select **Save Changes** to make the new picture your Desktop background.

2. Change the window and taskbar color.
   a) In the Personalization window, select **Color** to access the Color and Appearance window.

   Color
   Automatic

   b) Select a color from the array.
   c) Verify that the window borders and taskbar change to that color.
   d) Drag the **Color intensity** slider to change the intensity of the color.

   Color intensity:

   e) Confirm that the color of the borders and taskbar changes intensity.
   f) When you have adjusted the color and intensity to your liking, select **Save changes** to keep the changes and return to the Personalization window.

3. Select a screen saver.
   a) In the Personalization window, select **Screen Saver** to access the **Screen Saver Settings** dialog box.
   b) In the **Screen saver** section, verify that the **Screen saver** menu bar is set to **None**.

   Screen saver
   (None)   Settings...   Preview

   c) On the **Screen saver** menu bar, select the down arrow to view available screen savers.
   d) Select **Bubbles**.

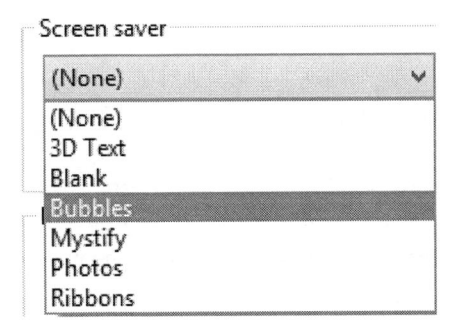

e) In the **Screen saver** section, select the **Preview** button to see how the screen saver will look on your screen.
f) To end preview, move your pointer or press any key.
g) On the **Screen saver** menu bar, select the down arrow and select the **3D Text** screen saver.
h) In the **Screen saver** section, select **Settings.**

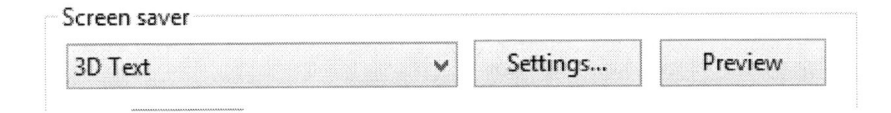

i) In the **3D Text Settings** dialog box, in the **Text** section, confirm that **Custom Text** is selected.
j) In the **Custom Text** text box, select **Windows 8** to highlight it.

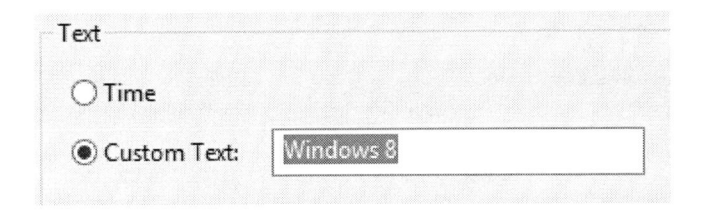

k) Type your name in the text box to replace Windows 8.
l) Select **OK.**
m) In the **Screen saver** section, select **Preview**.
n) Confirm that your name is now the screen saver.
o) Move your pointer to return to the **Screen Saver Settings** dialog box.
p) In the **Screen saver** section, in the **Wait** spin box, select the up and down arrows to change how long your PC needs to be idle before the screen saver is displayed.

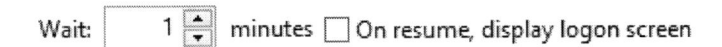

q) Select **OK** to save changes and close the **Screen Saver** dialog box.

4. Change the pointer shape.
   a) In the Personalization window **Navigation** pane, select **Change mouse pointers** to open the **Mouse Properties** dialog box.
   b) In the display box near the top right of the window, verify that the default pointer is shown.
   c) In the **Customize** box, scroll to view the current pointer shapes.
   d) In the **Schemes** section, on the **Scheme** menu bar, verify that **None** is listed.

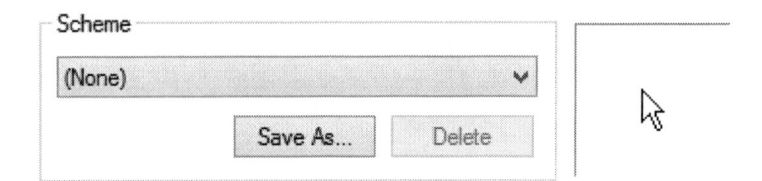

e) On the **Scheme** menu bar, select the down arrow to view a list of available pointer schemes.
f) From the list, select a pointer scheme option.
g) In the display box, verify that the pointer changes shape.
h) In the **Customize** box, confirm that the shapes have changed as well.
i) Select **Apply** to accept the new scheme.
j) Confirm that your pointer changes to the new shape.

> **Note:** If you wish to change the pointer back, on the **Schemes** menu bar, select **None**, and then select **Apply**.

5. Change pointer motion options.
   a) At the top of the dialog box, select **Pointer Options**.

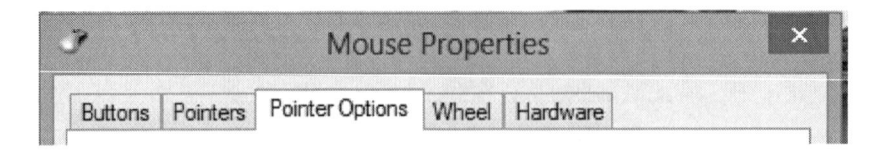

   b) In the **Motion** section, drag the **Motion** slider to **Slow**.
   c) Move your pointer around to verify that your pointer now moves more slowly in relation to your mouse movements.
   d) Drag the **Motion** slider to Fast and move your pointer to verify that it now moves faster.
   e) Drag the slider to a point you prefer.

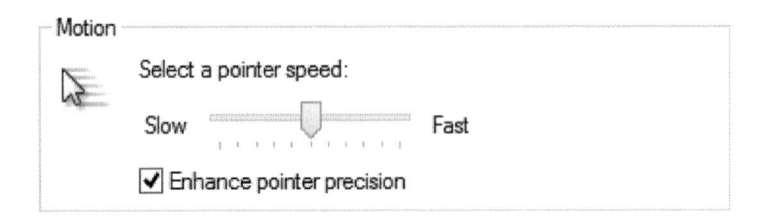

   f) In the **Visibility** section, check the **Display pointer trails** check box.
   g) Move your pointer.
   h) It is followed by a trail of pointers.

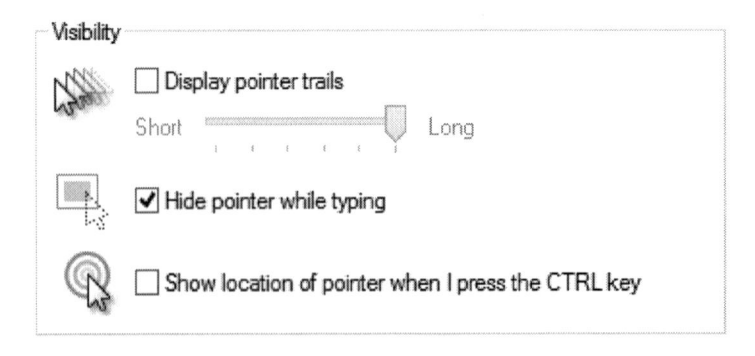

i) Uncheck **Display pointer trails** (you may skip this step if you like having the trails on).
j) Select **OK** to save changes and close the **Mouse Properties** dialog box.

6. Close the Personalization window and return to **Start.**

Summary

In this lesson, you identified ways to customize your PC so that it fits the way you work and reflects your personality. You also learned how to make your pointer easier to work with, how to make the layout of Start more efficient, and how to control the devices connected to your PC.

Why might you customize the look of your computer and pointer?

How might creating groups of tiles help you in your day-to-day work?

> **Note:** Check your LogicalCHOICE Course screen for opportunities to interact with your classmates, peers, and the larger LogicalCHOICE online community about the topics covered in this course or other topics you are interested in. From the Course screen you can also access available resources for a more continuous learning experience.

http://www.lo-choice.com

6 | Using Windows 8 Security Features

Lesson Time: 1 hour

Lesson Objectives

In this lesson, you will:

- Set privacy levels and set and change your passwords.
- Use Windows Defender.
- Open SkyDrive and upload a file.

Lesson Introduction

The security of your PC, data, and privacy are very important in today's world. With Microsoft® Windows® 8, you can manage your privacy and protect your PC from unauthorized access, store and back up your files, and even safely share your files with others.

TOPIC A

Set Privacy Levels and Passwords

As you saw earlier in the course, passwords can help keep your account protected. In addition to using passwords to protect the data on your PC, you can limit how other personal information is accessed.

Passwords

Although you use a password to protect your PC, hackers are relentless when it comes to trying to steal your information. Periodically changing your password can go a long way toward thwarting them. To give you more options for signing in, Windows 8 allows you to create a picture password or a PIN password for faster sign-in. The default sign-in for Windows 8 is the eight-character password. A picture password will replace that. If you create a PIN password, it will take precedence over both the regular password and the picture password. However, at sign-in, you can select which option you wish to use by opening the **Sign-in** options below the **Password** text box. To ensure that no one can change your password and lock you out, you must enter your current password whenever you make a password change.

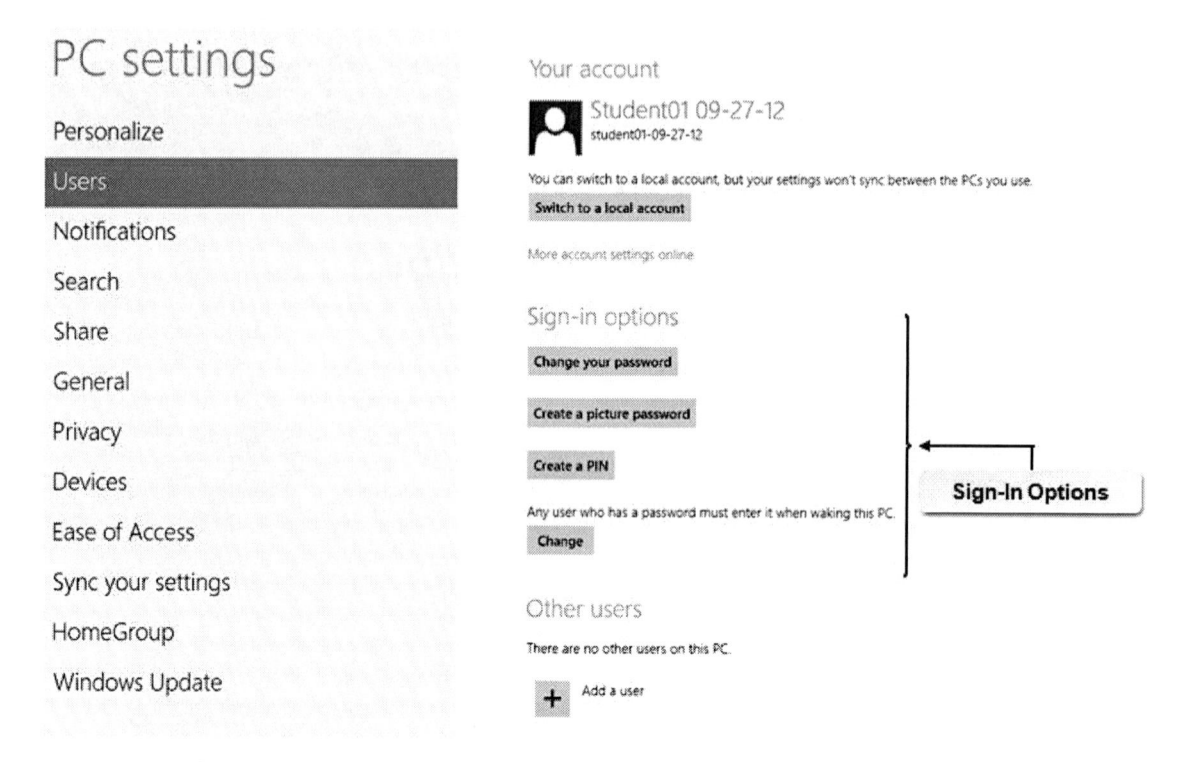

Figure 6-1: The sign-in options in PC settings.

PIN Passwords

PIN passwords are four numbers long, making signing in quicker and easier. When you use the PIN password, you type in the numbers, but do not need to press **Enter.** Once you type the last number, you are automatically signed in.

Picture Passwords

With the picture password, you specify the picture and "draw" motions on the picture as the password. These motions can be any combination of taps, straight lines, and circles; and the size, position, direction, and order in which you make the motions combine to become your password. Because some hackers use programs that record your keystrokes, giving them access to your eight-character password or four-digit PIN, the motions used in picture passwords offer another level of security.

Figure 6-2: Three gestures on a picture password.

Access the Checklist tile on your LogicalCHOICE course screen for reference information and job aids on How to Use Passwords

ACTIVITY 6-1
Changing Your Password

Data Files

C:\091102Data\Using Windows 8 Security Features\picture_password.png

Before You Begin

You are at the Start screen.

Scenario

To protect against data loss and identity theft, your company is now requiring employees to change their account passwords on a regular basis. You'll create a PIN password, change your current password, and create a picture password. You will then sign in using each of the new passwords. Knowing how to create and use all three types of passwords will enable you to vary your sign-in procedure and keep your data, identity, and PC better protected.

1. Create a PIN password.
    a) Select the **Settings Charm**.
    b) Select **Change PC settings**.
    c) In the **Navigation** pane of **PC settings**, select **Users**.

    PC settings

    Personalize

    Users

    d) Confirm that the **Contents** pane contains **Your Account** and **Sign-in options**.
    e) In the **Contents** pane, in the **Sign-in options** section, select **Create a PIN**.

    Sign-in options

    Change your password

    Create a picture password

    Create a PIN

    f) Verify that the **Create a PIN** screen is displayed.

g) On the **Create a PIN** screen, in the **Password** text box, enter *win8class*

![Create a PIN dialog showing "First, confirm your current password." with Student account and password field containing win8class, with OK and Cancel buttons]

h) In the **Enter PIN** text box, type *1234*
i) In the **Confirm PIN** text box, type *1234*

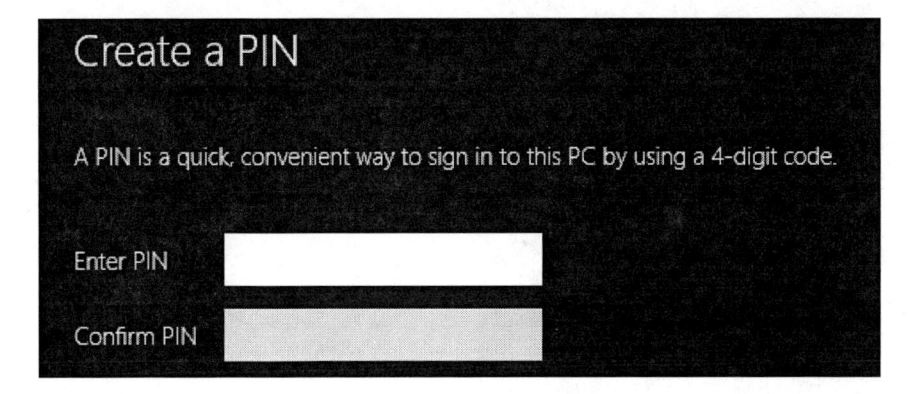

![Create a PIN screen: "A PIN is a quick, convenient way to sign in to this PC by using a 4-digit code." with Enter PIN and Confirm PIN fields]

j) Select **Finish**.

> **Note:** When you do this on your PC, it's a good idea to use random numbers to make it harder for a hacker to figure out. For our purposes here, 1234 is fine.

k) In the **Sign-in options** section, verify that there is now an option to **Remove the PIN**.
l) Verify that **Create a PIN** has changed to **Change PIN**.
m) Return to **Start**.
n) Using your **Account ID** menu, select **Lock**.
o) Select anywhere to display the **Sign-in** screen.
p) Confirm that the **Password** text box now says **PIN**.
q) In the **Password** text box, type *1234* to sign in.
r) Verify that you are signed in and are viewing the **Start** screen.

2. Change your password.
   a) Use the **Switcher** to navigate to **PC settings**.
   b) In the **Navigation** pane of **PC settings,** confirm that **Users** is selected.
   c) Confirm that the **Contents** pane contains **Your Account** and **Sign-in options**.
   d) In the **Contents** pane, select **Change your password** to open the **Change your password** screen.
   e) In the **Old password** text box, type *win8class*
   f) In the **New password** text box, type *Win8cl@ss*
   g) In the **Reenter password** text box, type *Win8cl@ss*
   h) If prompted, enter a password hint.
   i) Select **Next**.
   j) When prompted, select **Finish**.

3. Create a picture password.
   a) Confirm that you are looking at the **Users** screen in **PC settings.**
   b) In the **Contents** pane, select **Create a picture password.**
   c) On the **Create a picture password** screen, in the **Password** text box, type *Win8cl@ss*
   d) Select **OK**.
   e) Confirm that you are viewing the **Welcome to picture password** screen.
   f) Observe that the motions shown on the example picture are a line, a circle, and a tap.
   g) Select **Choose picture** to open your **Pictures** library.

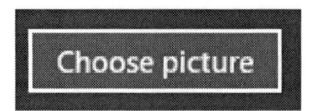

   h) In the **Pictures** library, select the **Butterfly** picture.

   i) Select **Open.**
   j) If necessary, drag the picture to position it so you can see both wings.
   k) Select **Use this picture**.

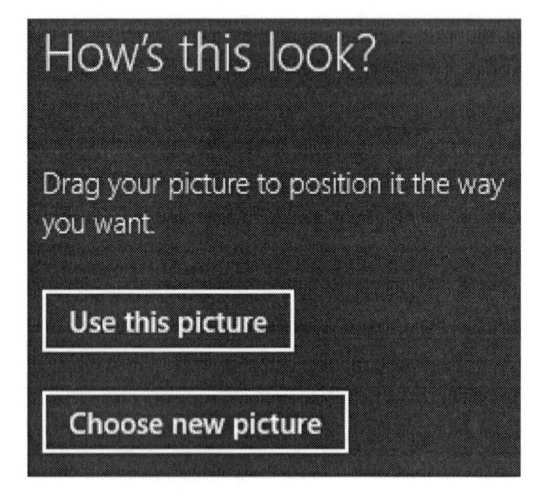

   l) Starting at the top of the right wing, drag your pointer toward the body, along the vertical line of yellow dots.
   m) Starting at the top of the left wing, drag your pointer toward the body, along the upper line of yellow dots.

n) Starting at the head of the butterfly, drag your pointer along the body toward the orange spots.
   o) When prompted, repeat the three gestures in order to confirm them. If you make a mistake, select **Try Again.**
   p) Select **Finish** to go back to **PC settings**.

4. Sign in using your new picture password.
   a) Return to **Start.**
   b) Using your **Account ID** menu, select **Lock**.
   c) Select anywhere to display the **Sign-in** screen.
   d) Confirm that your picture appears, along with the option to switch to your password.
   e) Select **Switch to password**.
   f) Below the **Password** text box, select **Sign-in options.**
   g) Confirm that the options show three icons: a picture of mountains, a key, and a pin pad.
   h) Select the pin pad.
   i) Verify that the password text box now says **PIN**.
   j) Select the mountains icon.
   k) You are taken to the picture password screen.
   l) Draw your three gestures on the butterfly to sign in. If you make a mistake, you can select **Start Over** and try again.
   m) Verify that you are returned to the **Start** screen.

Privacy

Although allowing websites to track your location can give you a more tailored online experience, there will be times when you will want to maintain your privacy. Along with limiting access to location, you can decide whether or not apps can use your name and account picture, and whether to let Microsoft keep track of what websites you visit for use in determining what apps to provide in the Windows Store. Although you may trust some websites to keep your personal information protected, other sites may not be as trustworthy, and denying access to your information is one step toward protecting yourself.

Privacy

Let apps use my location
On

Let apps use my name and account picture
On

Help improve Windows Store by sending URLs for the web content that apps use
On

Privacy statement

Figure 6-3: The Privacy menu options.

> Access the Checklist tile on your LogicalCHOICE course screen for reference information and job aids on **How to Change Privacy Settings**.

ACTIVITY 6-2
Changing Privacy Settings

Scenario

Due to ongoing security concerns, your company is limiting how employees share information. Controlling how your information is used is another step in protecting your identity. You will change your privacy settings to disable name, account picture, and web use information sharing.

Access privacy settings and disable sharing.
a) Select the **Settings Charm**.
b) Select **Change PC settings**.
c) In the **Navigation** pane, select **Privacy.**
d) If necessary, select the toggle for **Let apps use my location** to turn it **Off**.

> Let apps use my location
> Off

e) If necessary, select the toggle for **Let apps use my name and account picture** to turn it **Off**.

> Let apps use my name and account picture
> Off

f) If necessary, select the toggle for **Help improve Windows Store** to turn it **Off**.

> Help improve Windows Store by sending URLs for the web content that apps use
> Off

g) Verify that there is a Windows 8 Privacy Statement link. This is a link to Microsoft's online privacy statement.
h) Return to **Start.**

TOPIC B

Use Windows Defender

While the Internet is an amazing tool, which provides you with access to an astounding amount of content, there are also dangers associated with surfing the web. Without even knowing it, you can infect your computer with malicious software and other dangerous elements. In order to productively benefit from the resources available online, you need to ensure your computer is safe from threats. Windows 8 comes loaded with built-in protection against such threats: Widows Defender. Understanding how use this security tool can help ease your mind as you take advantage of everything the Internet has to offer.

Windows Defender

Whenever you connect to the Internet or open email from unknown senders, your computer is vulnerable to viruses, malicious software (malware), spyware, and unwanted pop-up windows. Many of these unwanted programs can steal the information on your computer, record your keystrokes (a way of recording your passwords), cause damage to your computer, and slow the performance of your PC. *Windows Defender* is a free Microsoft program that protects your computer from unwanted software downloads, and removes and quarantines any that it finds on your hard drive. It is a good idea to run Windows Defender to create a *restore point* while everything is working well on your computer, and routinely update that restore point. This enables you to restore your computer to a working point if it becomes infected with unwanted software.

You can have Windows Defender **Real-time protection** running in the background, so that whenever any unwanted software tries to install itself on your computer, you will be alerted. Many times, viruses are attached to email, and users unwittingly download them when they open these attachments. **Real-time protection** scans attachments and alerts you when it finds anything suspicious. Because hackers are constantly creating new versions of these programs, Windows Defender automatically updates new definitions of potentially dangerous software. When Windows 8 is installed, Windows Defender is on by default.

> **Note:** Windows Defender is turned on or off for the PC, so if you have multiple accounts and one user turns it off, it is off for all accounts on that PC.

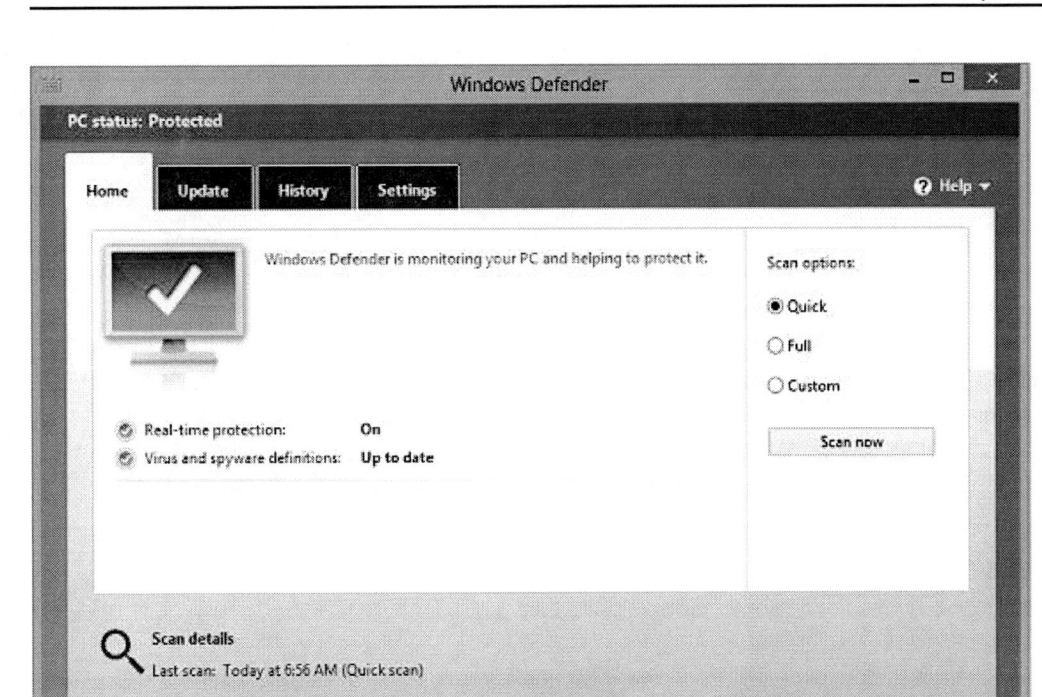

Figure 6-4: Windows Defender.

> Access the Checklist tile on your LogicalCHOICE course screen for reference information and job aids on **How to Use Windows Defender**

ACTIVITY 6-3
Changing Windows Defender Settings

Scenario
There may be times when you find that your PC has been running a bit slow, or you need to change some of the settings in Windows Defender to customize your protection, to scan removable devices, or create a restore point. You will open Windows Defender, identify the options available, and run a quick scan. Knowing how to work with Windows Defender will help keep your PC and the data it contains protected.

1. Open Windows Defender.
    a) Right-click the **Start** screen to open the command bar.
    b) On the command bar, select the **All Apps** icon.
    c) On the **All Apps** screen, under the **Windows System** programs, select **Windows Defender** to open the program.

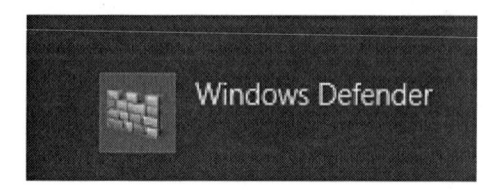

    d) Verify that Windows Defender opens on the Desktop.
    e) In the Windows Defender window, observe the tabs: **Home, Update, History,** and **Settings.**

2. Determine the status of your protection.
    a) If necessary, select the **Home** tab.
    b) Verify that **Real-time protection** is on.
    c) Verify that your virus and spyware definitions are up-to-date.

    > Real-time protection: On
    > Virus and spyware definitions: Up to date

    d) Identify the scan options. Hold your pointer over the scan options to view the pop-up description.
    e) On the bottom of the **Home** tab, identify the time and type of the last scan run.

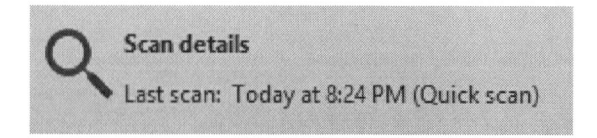

    > Scan details
    > Last scan: Today at 8:24 PM (Quick scan)

3. Identify the details of the last definitions update.
    a) Select the **Update** tab to view update status.
    b) Identify the date of the last virus definition creation.
    c) Identify the date of the last update.
    d) Identify the virus and spyware definition versions.

e) Identify the **Update** button.

Windows Defender updates your virus and spyware definitions automatically to help protect your PC.

Definitions created on:	10/8/2012 at 7:53 PM
Definitions last updated:	10/9/2012 at 4:56 AM
Virus definition version:	1.137.1371.0
Spyware definition version:	1.137.1371.0

Update

4. Confirm settings.
   a) Select the **Settings** tab.
   b) If necessary, in the **Navigation** pane, select **Real-time protection**.
   c) Verify that **Turn on Real time protection** is checked.
   d) In the **Navigation** pane, select **Advanced.**
   e) Identify the actions that can be taken on this menu.
   f) In the **Navigation** pane, select **Administrator.**
   g) Verify that **Turn on Windows Defender** is checked.

5. (Optional) Run a quick scan.
   a) Select the **Home** tab.
   b) Under **Scan options,** select **Quick.**
   c) Select the **Scan now** button to begin the scan.
   d) Observe the number of items scanned.

6. Close the Windows Defender window and return to **Start.**

TOPIC C

Store and Share Files with SkyDrive

In your work, you've probably needed to share files with your coworkers, or taken a document home to work on it. With SkyDrive, you'll have more flexibility in how you accomplish that.

SkyDrive

You've probably heard people talking about the *"cloud"* and *"cloud computing"* and wondered what it was all about. Basically, when you access the cloud, you are making use of hardware and software computing resources that are available over the Internet. The term *cloud* is used as a metaphor to give people an easy-to-understand image of the infrastructure of the Internet. Cloud storage services, such as Microsoft *SkyDrive*, typically charge fees based on how much storage space you wish to use, and many give you a certain amount of space for free to get you started. SkyDrive comes bundled with Windows 8 and is configured with three folders: **Documents, Pictures**, and **Public.** You can add more folders as needed. To use SkyDrive, you need to have a Microsoft Account.

> **Note:** Microsoft Accounts are discussed in the Appendix.

You can access your files on SkyDrive from your PC, smartphone, or by signing in to your SkyDrive account from any computer. When you download a file from SkyDrive, it will check to see if there is already a file in the destination folder with the same name. If so, SkyDrive will add a number after the name of the file it downloads to prevent accidentally overwriting the existing file.

When you open a file on SkyDrive from your PC, it will be opened using the appropriate program. Files stored on SkyDrive are read only, so if you make changes to a file, you must save it under a different name and designate a destination folder. However, when you open a SkyDrive file from another PC, a copy of the file will be downloaded to that PC, and you can edit and save that copy. SkyDrive also allows you to share files by using the **Share Charm,** or by creating a group and inviting others to the group.

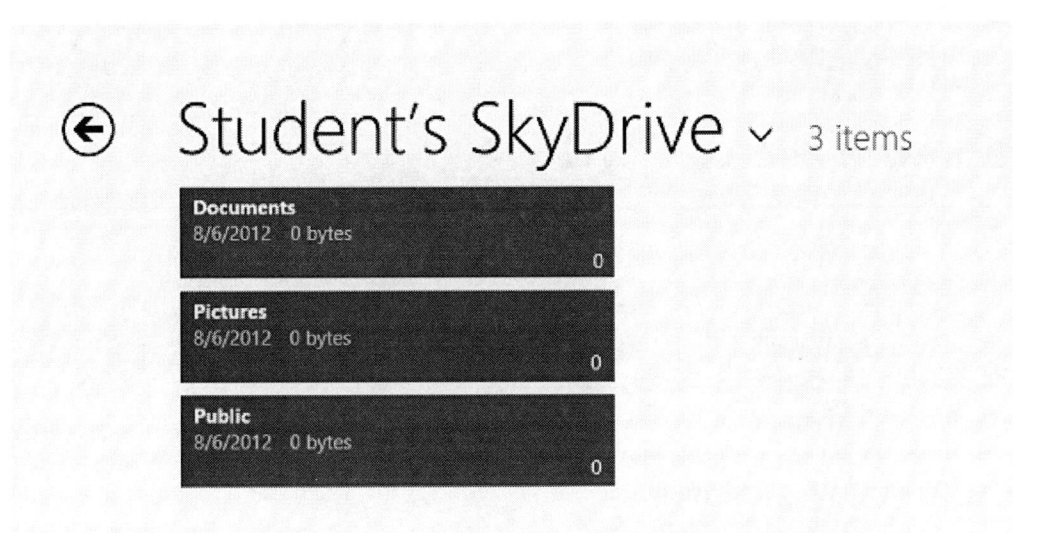

Figure 6-5: SkyDrive folders.

	Access the Checklist tile on your LogicalCHOICE course screen for reference information and job aids on How to Use SkyDrive

ACTIVITY 6-4
Uploading a File to SkyDrive

Scenario
There may be times at work when you need to take a document or picture home with you to work on, or you may want to share a file with a coworker or colleague. Uploading it to SkyDrive will give you that flexibility. You will upload the Tents file to the Documents folder on SkyDrive. Then you will download the file, make changes to it, and save it on your PC.

1. Upload the **Tents** document to SkyDrive.
    a) Select the **SkyDrive** tile to open the app.

    b) If necessary, sign in with your assigned Microsoft Account username and password.
    c) Verify that it contains three empty folders.
    d) Select the **Documents** folder.

    e) Right-click to display the command bar.
    f) Observe the options. You can refresh the page, create a new folder, upload a file, change the way items are presented, and select all items in the folder.

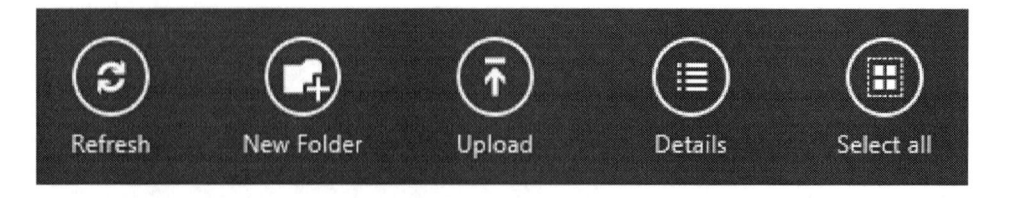

    g) Select **Upload** to open the **Files selection** page.
    h) Verify that it shows the files and folders contained in your **Documents** library.

i) Next to **Files,** select the down arrow to view the locations on your computer where you can search for files to upload.
j) Select outside the menu to close it.

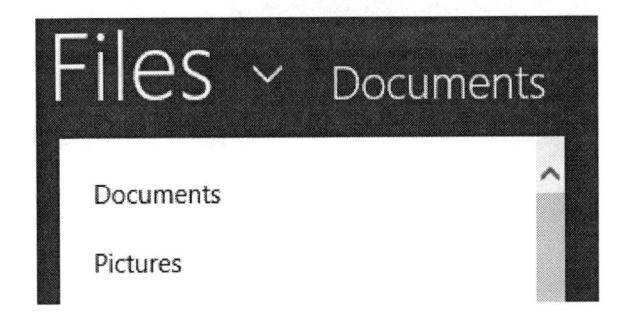

k) Verify that the **Documents** library is still displayed.
l) Select the **Letters** folder to open it.
m) Select the **Tents** file.

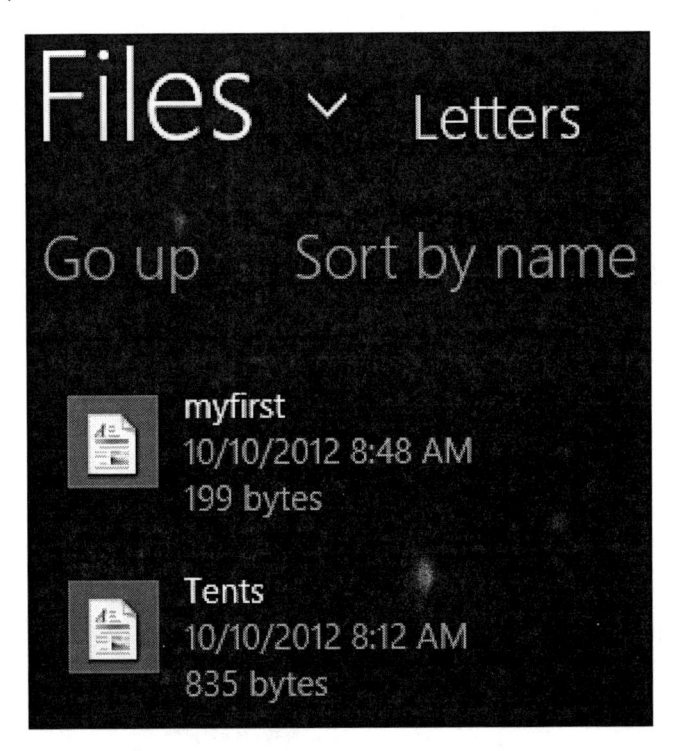

n) Select **Add to SkyDrive** to begin uploading the file.

o) Verify that the **Tents** file is now in the SkyDrive **Documents** folder.
p) Confirm that the command bar is still visible.

2. Download a file from SkyDrive.
    a) Right-click the **Tents** file to access additional command bar options.
    b) Select **Download**.

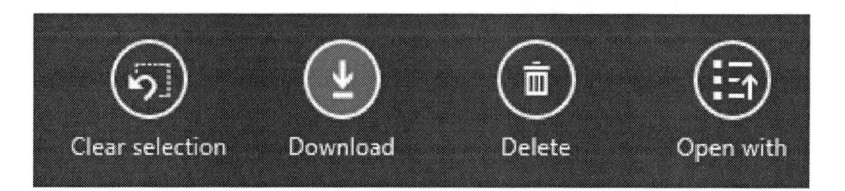

    c) On the **Files selection** page, select the **Letters** folder. This will be the destination folder.
    d) Select **Choose this folder**.

    e) In the bottom-left corner of your screen, verify that the destination folder **Letters** is displayed.
    f) Select **OK** to confirm the download.

3. Locate the files in File Explorer.
    a) Access the Desktop app.
    b) Open File Explorer.
    c) In the **Documents** library, open the **Letters** folder.
    d) Verify that the **Letters** folder contains three files: **myfirst, Tents**, and the downloaded file **Tents (2)**.

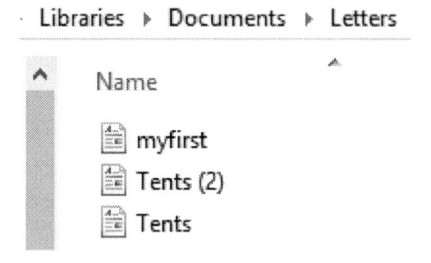

4. Close File Explorer.

5. Shut down the computer.
    a) Open the **Settings Charm.**
    b) Select the **Power** icon.
    c) Select **Shut down** to close your account and turn off the computer.

Summary

In this lesson, you examined how to protect your PC against unauthorized access using alternative passwords, how to change your privacy settings, and how to use Windows Defender to protect against viruses and spyware. You also used SkyDrive to upload and download files. Using these methods, you'll be better prepared to protect against theft and have more flexibility when sharing and accessing your data.

Why do you think Windows 8 gives password options such as a PIN and pictures? Do you think you might use a picture password at work? Why?

What might be the advantages of using SkyDrive? How do you think you might use it in your job?

> **Note:** Check your LogicalCHOICE Course screen for opportunities to interact with your classmates, peers, and the larger LogicalCHOICE online community about the topics covered in this course or other topics you are interested in. From the Course screen you can also access available resources for a more continuous learning experience.

http://www.lo-choice.com

Course Follow-up

In this course, you identified the components of a personal computer and used the mouse to move about the screen. You examined Windows 8 apps and used the live tiles to open those apps. You also discovered the difference between Modern apps and Desktop applications. You used the Charms to search within apps and online, and examined how the Share Charm enables you to send information to your coworkers. You found out how SkyDrive can give you more flexibility in storing and using your files, and saw how to protect your PC using passwords and Windows Defender. With this knowledge, you will be able to begin using your Windows 8 PC at work and at home.

What's Next?

You are encouraged to explore Windows 8 and related applications further. If you wish to learn more about word processing, spreadsheets, or other applications, Logical Operations has a full offering of courses for the beginning and advanced student. Some that might interest you include courses for Microsoft Office 2010, (including Microsoft® Office Excel® 2010: Part 1, Microsoft® Office Word 2010: Part 1, Microsoft® Office PowerPoint® 2010: Part 1, and Microsoft® Office Outlook® 2010: Part 1), as well as a full offering for Microsoft Office 2013 (including Microsoft® Office Excel® 2013: Part 1, Microsoft® Office Word 2013: Part 1, Microsoft® Office PowerPoint® 2013: Part 1, and Microsoft® Office Outlook® 2013: Part 1). Take whichever track suits the version of Office you work with the most.

> **Note:** Check your LogicalCHOICE Course screen for opportunities to interact with your classmates, peers, and the larger LogicalCHOICE online community about the topics covered in this course or other topics you are interested in. From the Course screen you can also access available resources for a more continuous learning experience.

A | Other Windows 8 Features

Appendix Introduction

Microsoft® Windows® 8 allows multiple accounts on one PC, and you can add and delete users as needed. Windows 8 also offers a couple of ways of sharing, storing, and backing up your files. Along with SkyDrive®, File History enables you to back up and restore your files, providing you with peace of mind.

TOPIC A

Create a New User Account

Windows 8 allows you to have more than one account on your PC, whether they are Microsoft Accounts, or Local Accounts. Although you can use many of the apps and features of Windows 8 with a Local Account, accessing all that Windows 8 offers requires setting up a Microsoft Account.

Microsoft Account

With a Microsoft Account, you can download apps from the Microsoft Store, access online accounts such as SkyDrive automatically, and sync multiple PCs so that they look and feel the same. If you have a Hotmail® account or a Windows Live ID, you already have a Microsoft Account. You can use Windows 8 without a Microsoft Account by creating a Local Account, but you will be required to sign in when accessing some of the online features, and you will not be able to sync your computers.

Local Account

With a Local Account, you will still be able to use Desktop applications, go online, and use some of the Modern apps on your PC. You can also download applications from the Internet, or load them from a disk. However, you won't be able to use the Mail, Calendar, Messaging, People, and SkyDrive apps provided by Windows 8. Most of these, however, have equivalent programs that are available online. And, unlike with a Microsoft Account, you won't be able to sync, or automatically setup, other PCs to look and act like your primary PC, nor will you be able to download any apps from the Microsoft Store. If you set up your account as a Local Account, you can always change it to a Microsoft Account later.

> **Access the Checklist tile on your LogicalCHOICE course screen for reference information and job aids on How to Create a Microsoft Account**

TOPIC B

File History

Once you have accumulated a number of files, or have files that are irreplaceable, backing up your data becomes very important. While the cloud is good for storing files you'd like to use on the go or with other computers, it can be quite expensive to store large quantities of data, and accidental deletions and changes can take place.

File History in Windows 8

It's always a good idea to have a backup, or a copy of your data kept in storage off of your PC, as insurance against accidental deletion, or in cases where your computer breaks or is lost. However, because most of us forget to make backups, or don't do it in a timely fashion, Windows 8 comes with File History, which automatically backs up your files. To ensure your files are safely stored off of your computer, File History requires you to use an external storage device or a network drive. Once File History is turned on and your storage device is designated, it will run in the background, saving the different versions of your files from your libraries, Desktop, contacts, and favorites automatically. If you use an external storage device, you must leave it attached to your PC for File History to automatically back up your files. If you choose to, you can specify folders to exclude from your backup, specify how often backups are created, or begin a manual backup. To restore a backed up version of a file, open File History and use the **Restore personal files** function.

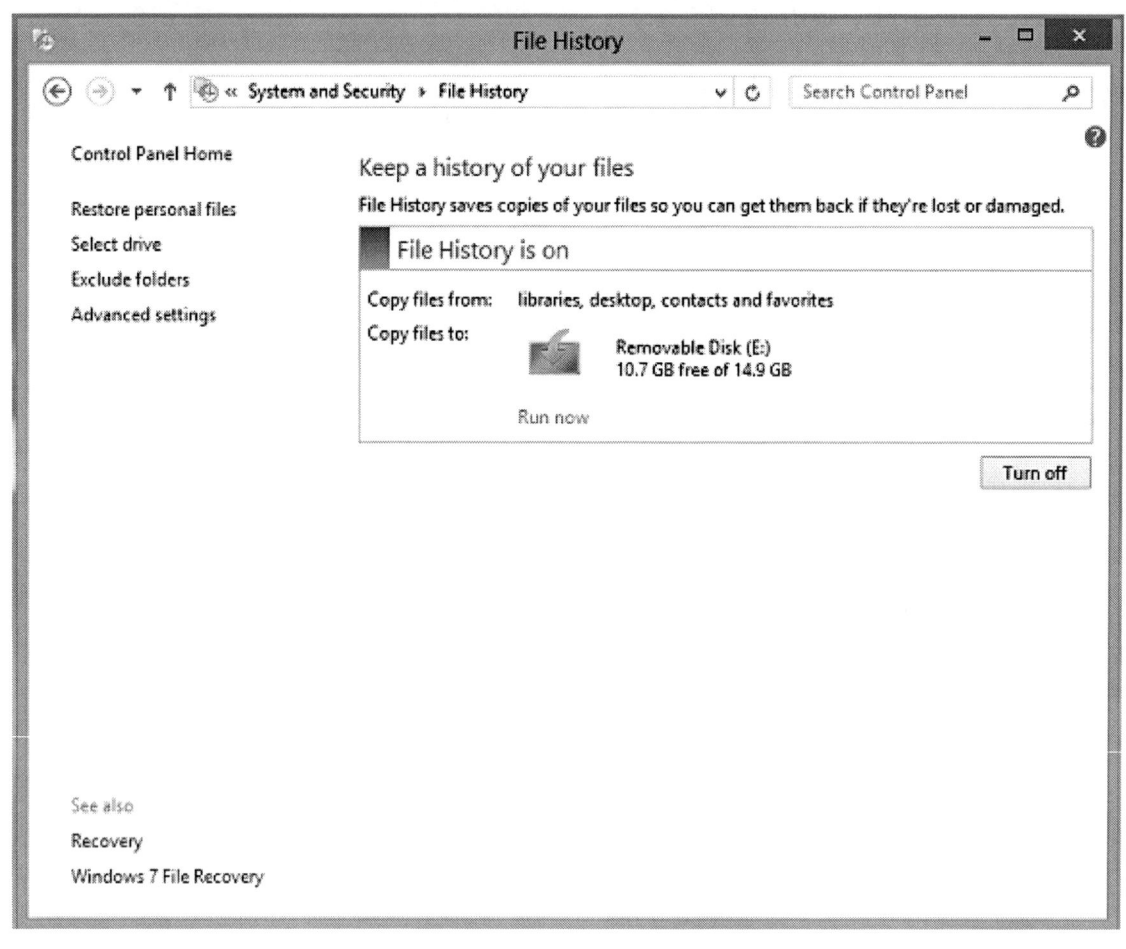

Figure A-1: File History.

> Access the Checklist tile on your LogicalCHOICE course screen for reference information and job aids on How to Use File History

Lesson Labs

Lesson labs are provided as an additional learning resource for this course. The labs may or may not be performed as part of the classroom activities. Your instructor will consider setup issues, classroom timing issues, and instructional needs to determine which labs are appropriate for you to perform, and at what point during the class. If you do not perform the labs in class, your instructor can tell you if you can perform them independently as self-study, and if there are any special setup requirements.

Lesson Lab 1-1
Managing Tiles and the Start Screen

Activity Time: 15 minutes

Before You Begin
Microsoft Office is installed.

Scenario
Your company just made the switch from Windows 7 to Windows 8. Your IT department has installed Microsoft Office on all employee computers, and has migrated all contacts and files, and as many settings as possible to the new setup. You have reviewed all of your files and are satisfied that you have everything you need. However, you want to set up you Windows 8 environment to accommodate your typical work flow. So, you decide to rearrange the tiles on the **Start** screen, pin your commonly used applications to the **Start** screen, and personalize your background and account picture.

---

1. Arrange the Modern app tiles so that the following tiles make up the first column on the **Start** screen: Mail, Desktop, News, Finance, Calendar, Weather.

2. Turn off all live tiles.

3. Make a small tile larger, and a large tile smaller.

4. Ensure all Microsoft Office tiles are pinned to the **Start** screen.

5. Use the semantic zoom feature to move the group of Microsoft Office application tiles to the left of all other tiles on the **Start** screen.

6. Add or change your account picture.

Lesson Lab 3-1
Managing Files and Libraries

Activity Time: 15 minutes

Data Files
C:\091102Data\Working with Desktop Applications\palm trees.JPG
C:\091102Data\Working with Desktop Applications\rio.JPG
C:\091102Data\Working with Desktop Applications\swiss alps.JPG

Scenario
You are a photographer who specializes in location photography for travel publications, international businesses, and marketing firms. You recently switched to Windows 8 and are excited about the addition of the ribbon to File Explorer. You have been storing your files in a folder at the root level of your hard drive, but feel it will be easier to manage the large number of image files you regularly work with by placing them within a folder in your My Documents folder. You decide to create a folder there, and then to begin the process of moving your image files to the new folder.

1. In File Explorer, navigate to the **My Documents** folder, and then create a folder named "images."

2. Using the File Explorer ribbon, copy and paste the palm trees.JPG file to the new **images** folder.

3. Using the File Explorer ribbon, move the rio.JPG and swiss alps.JPG files to the **images** folder.

4. Verify the images display in the **images** folder.

5. Close File Explorer.

Lesson Lab 4-1
Using IE 10

Activity Time: 15 minutes

Scenario
You are a television reporter for a local station in a relatively large metropolitan area. As such, you often cover news stories that deal with national, and even international, events. Your station just started using Windows 8, mainly to accommodate new mobile devices for reporters and video journalists. You want to get your desktop PC set up with all of the tools you are used to using on a daily basis. One of your top priorities is creating links to many of the news sites you use to research regional, national, and international news. You decide to save the links as tiles to the **Start** screen for quick access.

1. Launch IE to in the Modern UI.

2. Navigate to http://www.cnn.com/ and pin the website to the **Start** screen.

3. Search for and pin a second website to the **Start** screen.
   a) Open a new tab.
   b) Navigate to http://www.bing.com/ and perform a web search for the Fox News website.
   c) Follow a link to the site, and then pin it to the **Start** screen.

4. Close all tabs.

5. Pin another site to the **Start** screen, and then add it to your favorites.
   a) Navigate to http://www.bbc.com/.
   b) Pin the website to the **Start** screen.
   c) Add the site to your **Favorites** list.

6. Verify the new sites display in the **Quick Site Access Panel**.

7. Switch to the desktop version of Internet Explorer, and then verify that the BBC Web site displays in the **Favorites** menu.

   > **Note:** You may have to display the Menu bar in the desktop version of IE to verify this. To display the Menu bar, right click above the Address bar in the IE window, and then select **Menu bar** from the pop-up menu.

8. Close both the desktop and the Modern versions of IE 10.

9. If necessary, navigate to the **Start** screen and verify the links work from the newly added tiles, and then close IE 10.

Lesson Lab 6-1
Using Windows 8 Security Features

Activity Time: 15 minutes

Data Files
C:\091102Data\Using Windows 8 Security Features\food.jpg

Scenario
You are the General Manager of one location for a casual dining restaurant chain. You have received an email from the IT department indicating a number of company computers have been infected with a virus, and the situation may have been initiated by an employee of the company. The IT department has directed you to run a virus scan using Windows Defender and switch to using a 4-digit PIN or a picture password until they can determine which password was compromised and perform a password reset.

1. Run a Quick scan using Windows Defender.
    a) From the **Start** screen, use instant search to find and launch Windows Defender.
    b) Run a Quick scan.
    c) Close Windows Defender.

2. Set a 4-Digit PIN.
    a) Access the **PC setting** screen.
    b) Select the **Users** tab, and then set a 4-Digit PIN.
    c) Record your 4-digit PIN here:_____.
    d) Verify the 4-Digit PIN has been set by signing out, and then signing back in using the 4-digit PIN.

3. Set a picture password.
    a) Access the **PC settings** screen.
    b) Select the **Users** tab, and then set a picture password using the food.jpg image.
    c) Record your three gestures here:_____.
    d) Verify the picture password has been set by signing out, and then signing back in using the picture password.

Solutions

ACTIVITY 1-1: Identifying Personal Computer Components and Applications

---

1. Which type of software would be best for gathering and sorting through the large amount of data contained in the surveys? Why?
   - ○ Spreadsheet
   - ○ Word processor
   - ◉ Database
   - ○ Presentation

2. If you want to type up a report and create a slide show, which two types of software would you use?
   - ☐ Spreadsheet
   - ☑ Word processor
   - ☐ Database
   - ☑ Presentation

3. What is the purpose of the operating system?
   - ○ To create spreadsheets
   - ◉ To create a work environment for application software
   - ○ To process data from a database
   - ○ To share data in documents

4. How are desktop PCs, laptops, and tablets similar?

   A: Answers may include: they all have hardware, software, and operating systems; they all have input, processing, and output devices.

5. How are desktop PCs, laptops, and tablets different?

   A: Answers may include: the size of units; portability; laptops and tablets have input, processing, and output in one unit, whereas a desktop is made up of separate devices. Some use a mouse and keyboard, others use touch screen.

6. What types of applications might you use for your daily work?

A: Answers will vary depending on the user's needs, but may include word processor, spreadsheet, database, presentation, project management, educational, business, or industrial applications.

Glossary

app
A Windows 8 Modern User Interface style software application.

application icon
A small labeled picture on the Desktop that acts as a shortcut for running a program.

body
The portion of the window where work is displayed. The body of directory windows include the Navigation pane and Content pane.

boot
When the PC is turned on, the process of self-tests it performs before loading the operating system.

Charms
Context-sensitive tools available from everywhere in Windows 8 that provide access to system-wide functions.

Clipboard
The element that stores cut or copied text or images and enables them to be pasted or moved within a document or to another application.

cloud computing
The use of software and hardware resources that are delivered as a service over the Internet.

context menu
A menu displayed when right-clicking application icons, the taskbar, and the Desktop that provides quick access to common tasks. Also called jump lists.

Desktop
A Windows 8 app that provides an environment for running classic Windows software applications, as well as performing system functions like file management, Control Panel access, Windows Defender, File History, and so forth.

Desktop application
A software application designed to run in a traditional Microsoft window on the Desktop.

drag
Move your pointer over an item on your screen, and press and hold the left mouse button as you move the mouse. Release the button when the item has been moved to the desired location.

File Explorer
The Windows 8 component used to view and manage the computer's filing system.

folder
A directory used to store files.

Internet portal
A website that gathers information from many sources to present it on a single site.

keyboard shortcut
Keys or key combinations used to execute a menu command.

library
A directory similar to a folder that does not store files but instead tracks where files and folders are located and presents them in a single area.

live tiles
A tile that displays real-time information, even when the app is not running.

Modern app
A software application designed to run in the new application environment introduced with Windows 8.

Notification area
The right side of the taskbar that displays icons for system functions and shows messages about computer issues.

reboot
The process of turning the PC off and back on to apply any updates and perform clean-up procedures.

Recycle Bin
The directory that stores deleted folders and files. Folders and files can be restored to their original locations until the Recycle Bin is emptied.

restore point
A user-specified healthy computer state that can be returned to in the event that it becomes infected with malicious software.

ribbon
The interface element that includes tabs and commands for managing, editing, and viewing files.

screen saver
A feature that displays a blank screen or series of pictures after a period of computer inactivity.

SkyDrive
The Microsoft cloud-computing solution bundled with Windows 8. It enables users to store, and access files from any equipped computer.

Snap
A feature to show two apps on the same screen at once.

snap bar
The dividing line between two snapped apps that can be dragged to change the size of the apps.

Switcher
An interface element used to flip between open apps.

taskbar
The element along the bottom of the screen that displays icons for open or pinned apps.

tile
A graphic box, containing text and/or graphics, that represents a Windows 8 app and provides a means of opening the app it represents. Some tiles can also show preview information about the app in "live tile" mode.

tooltip
A hint that displays the name or function of a tile, icon, or menu option when you hover your pointer over the item.

URL
(Uniform Resource Locator) The unique address for a website on the Internet.

web browser
A program that locates and displays information on the World Wide Web.

Windows Defender
A built-in program that protects Windows computers from malicious software and unwanted downloads.

Index

A

Account ID menu *18*
All Apps screen *13*
app command bar *13*
apps
    Close App function *35*
    Desktop applications *12*
    Modern apps *12*, *28*
    multiple-app functionality *34*
    types of *3*

B

Bing
    Popular Now pane *77*
body of the window *60*
booting *6*
browsing preferences *85*

C

Charms
    Settings Charm *97*
    Share Charm *85*
    Start screen *24*
Clipboard *65*
cloud *126*
cloud computing *126*
Context menus *43*

D

Desktop
    application icons *44*
    background *104*
    Personalization window *104*

Desktop windows
    elements of *58*
    managing *60*
dialog boxes *51*
documents
    create new *65*
    open existing *65*
    save *65*

E

Ease of Access Menu
    features *8*

F

File Explorer *49*
folders *49*

H

hardware components *2*

I

IE10
    command bar *82*
    Search bar *82*
    Tabs menu *84*
    using search suggestions *82*
Internet Explorer 10, *See* IE10
internet portal *76*

K

keyboard shortcuts *43*

L

libraries *49*
Lock screen *6*

N

Notification area *43*

O

operating system, *See* OS
OS *3*

P

passwords
    picture *9, 115*
    PIN *9, 114*
    requirements *9*
PC Settings menu *97*
Pointers *105*
Print *66*
privacy menu *119*

Q

Quick Access Toolbar *59*
Quick Site Access Panel *83*

R

reboot *6*
Recycle Bin *51*
Redo *66*
restore point *122*
ribbon *50*

S

screen savers *105*
scroll bar *15*
search categories menu *78*
search engines
    examples of *76*
Shut Down menu *9*
Sign In screen *7*
SkyDrive
    Share Charm *126*
Snap feature
    Snap bar *34*
Start button *14*
Start screen *12*
Switcher *34*

T

taskbar *43*
Tile Groups *94*
tiles
    dragging *12*
    Live tiles *13*
tooltips *12, 43*

U

Undo *66*
Uniform Resource Locator, *See* URL
URL *76*

W

web browsers
    examples of *76*
Windows Defender
    Real-time protection *122*